Write it Right

Palgrave Study Guides

Authoring a PhD
Career Skills
Critical Thinking Skills
e-Learning Skills
Effective Communication for
  Arts and Humanities Students
Effective Communication for
  Science and Technology
The Foundations of Research
The Good Supervisor
How to Manage your Arts, Humanities and
  Social Science Degree
How to Manage your Distance and
  Open Learning Course
How to Manage your Postgraduate Course
How to Manage your Science and
  Technology Degree
How to Study Foreign Languages
How to Write Better Essays
IT Skills for Successful Study
Making Sense of Statistics
The Mature Student's Guide to Writing
The Postgraduate Research Handbook

Presentation Skills for Students
The Principles of Writing in Psychology
Professional Writing
Research Using IT
Skills for Success
The Student Life Handbook
The Palgrave Student Planner
The Student's Guide to Writing (2nd edn)
The Study Skills Handbook (2nd edn)
Study Skills for Speakers of English as
  a Second Language
Studying the Built Environment
Studying Economics
Studying History (2nd edn)
Studying Mathematics and its Applications
Studying Modern Drama (2nd edition)
Studying Physics
Studying Programming
Studying Psychology
Teaching Study Skills and Supporting Learning
Work Placements – a Survival Guide for Students
Write it Right
Writing for Engineers (3rd edn)

Palgrave Study Guides: Literature

General Editors: John Peck and Martin Coyle
How to Begin Studying English Literature
  (3rd edn)
How to Study a Jane Austen Novel (2nd edn)
How to Study a Charles Dickens Novel
How to Study Chaucer (2nd edn)
How to Study an E. M. Forster Novel
How to Study James Joyce
How to Study Linguistics (2nd edn)

How to Study Modern Poetry
How to Study a Novel (2nd edn)
How to Study a Poet
How to Study a Renaissance Play
How to Study Romantic Poetry (2nd edn)
How to Study a Shakespeare Play (2nd edn)
How to Study Television
Practical Criticism

Write it Right

A Handbook for Students

John Peck and Martin Coyle

First published 2005 by
PALGRAVE MACMILLAN
Houndmills, Basingstoke, Hampshire RG21 6XS and
175 Fifth Avenue, New York, N.Y. 10010
Companies and representatives throughout the world

PALGRAVE MACMILLAN is the global academic imprint of the Palgrave Macmillan division of St. Martin's Press, LLC and of Palgrave Macmillan Ltd. Macmillan® is a registered trademark in the United States, United Kingdom and other countries. Palgrave is a registered trademark in the European Union and other countries.

ISBN-13: 978 1–4039–9487–5
ISBN-10: 1–4039–9487–0

This book is printed on paper suitable for recycling and made from fully managed and sustained forest sources.

A catalogue record for this book is available from the British Library.

10 9 8 7 6 5 4 3 2 1
14 13 12 11 10 09 08 07 06 05

Printed in China

Contents

About this Book

It has often been pointed out that every diet book ever written could be reduced to one sentence: 'Eat less food, making sure it is the right kind of food.' We have written a book about how to write effectively, but the truth is that the entire secret of effective writing can be summed up in one sentence: 'Write shorter sentences, making sure the sentences are correctly punctuated.' That sounds easy enough. As everyone knows, however, writing clearly and correctly, especially in an essay, is always a challenge. There might be a few people with a natural gift for handling words, but most of us find it hard work.

As with so many activities in life, it helps if one gets the basics right. In the case of writing, this starts with being able to produce straightforward and correct sentences. Time and time again, the way of working out how to convey a complex point in an essay is to forget about writing a long and complicated sentence that covers the whole point in detail. Instead, explain the point step by step. Focus on producing a sequence of short sentences that conform to the basic rules of correct usage. The problem is that, by the time we are taking demanding examinations in a variety of subjects, most of us have forgotten a lot of the basic rules about correct usage.

It has always been the same. In the course of writing this book we looked at a large number of grammar and writing guides published over the course of the last hundred years. People a hundred years ago were making just the same mistakes that are made today, and, even more predictably, those who always complain about a decline in standards were, a hundred years ago, making just the same complaints about a decline in the standards of written English. Just when, we wonder, was this golden age when everyone emerged from primary school with a confident awareness of how to write perfect English?

The reason we looked at so many works about language skills was that we were conscious of a very real problem in trying to teach writing through the medium of a book. It might come as something of a surprise, but books about how to write are almost invariably badly written. We don't mean that the authors write ungrammatical sentences, but rather that, in chapter after chapter, they write in a way that fails to command the reader's attention. Grammar guides, in particular, tend to be full of hundreds of fragmentary examples and bewildering diagrams. Such guidance might be ideal if you are looking up the solution to a specific problem, but it is very difficult to concentrate over the course of several pages of such works. What everyone needs when they read any book is a narrative; they need, that is, something that sustains interest and carries them along. But how can this kind of narrative interest be sustained when dry rules are being expounded? It's a bit like the old joke about the telephone directory: great cast of characters, but not much of a plot. Indeed, our impression is that some grammar guides are so complicated that the reader is likely to know less, rather than more, after trying to read them.

We wouldn't dare, however, be so presumptuous as to claim that we have solved the problem of how to make a writing guide interesting and readable, but we have approached the task with some awareness of the problem involved. We have tried to create a work that might sustain the reader's interest, and which focuses on real issues: how to grasp the nature of the writing exercise you have embarked upon, how to organise your work in a logical and orderly way, and how to write literate sentences.

The book itself is organised into ten sections, which could be said to correspond to ten lectures in a university module. Each section is then divided into ten units; we have tried to make each of these units lively and self-sufficient in order to serve the needs of readers who just want to dip into the book on a casual basis. But each section is informed by one or more larger ideas, which are touched on in each unit within the section, and which are, essentially, the all-important ideas about how to write well. One way of putting all this is to say that, whereas the average writing guide is so bitty that the reader can't see the wood for trees, we have tried to offer a sense of the bigger picture; at each stage, we keep on returning to the informing principles of effective writing.

We are indebted to the many people who have helped make this book possible. Our biggest debt is to past and present students in the English Literature department at Cardiff University who over the years have taught us far more – both about literature and about writing – than we have ever managed to teach them. We have shamelessly plundered their essays, university applications, job applications, and their letters and emails to us, for examples of good and bad English; to save people's blushes, we have not given names, but this doesn't mean that we aren't extremely grateful to many, many students. It was reading students' essays, and, in particular, noticing what the good essays had in common, that brought us to a new kind of realisation of the importance of the main ideas that dominate this book.

The principal secret of effective writing is that it is, in every sense, simpler than you think. This starts with grasping the simple conventions that relate to the particular form of writing you have to undertake. Simplicity continues with the principle of relying as much as you can upon relatively short, but properly punctuated, sentences. A sentence never needs to expand and sprawl in order to say something complicated; it is much better to say what you are attempting to say in several short, but very clear, sentences. And finally, it is always possible to establish a clear, simple and logical order as you proceed from paragraph to paragraph in a piece of writing. In the course of this book, it should become clear just how much it is possible to achieve on the basis of such simple premises.

There is, however, one rather odd aspect of a book about how to write; this is that, in order to provide illustrations of common errors, it necessarily has to include a great many ungrammatical sentences. The danger of this, of course, is that readers may look at such sentences and perhaps assume that they are examples of good usage. What we have done to avoid confusion is to place an asterisk at the start of incorrect sentences and before any other examples containing misleading errors. This is standard practice in grammar and style books, and although it can become irritating or visually distracting, it seemed necessary to follow this style wherever there was any risk of misunderstanding.

There are, finally, two other points we should mention. We have taken the view that what you are looking for as a reader of this book is guidance about how to write in a formally correct way. Some people object to the kind of emphasis we have placed on 'correctness' as old fashioned, arguing that it destroys creativity and the life flow of language. All that we can say in reply is that they themselves usually write in grammatical sentences, and that the best creative writers we have come across are almost as obsessional as we are about their formal use of language. We are the first to admit that there are other, perhaps more flexible ways of approaching writing, and other books will give different advice about the issues we deal with. Our concern, however, is to provide students with something they can make immediate use of and rely upon rather than be baffled by.

The second point is about the audience for this book. We did not want to write a book for just one set of students or with just one topic in mind. The book is about effective writing across the whole range of tasks that face all of us on a daily basis, from writing a letter to organising larger academic projects. What we suggest is that the same basic methods and principles apply in all these situations. The opening sections, therefore, deliberately deal with everyday activities and with tasks that you are probably familiar with (such as applying for a course), because they illustrate, in a very direct way, what is involved in all forms of writing. As should become apparent, the principles underlying one kind of writing can be transferred to any other type of writing. There is a simple reason why this is true: once you know how to write a sentence, you can do almost anything with words. That is the joy of language.

About the title

'The boy played brilliant.' This is football-speak, the way that managers talk about their players. Those who have been fortunate enough to receive a good education – and perhaps with a touch of resentment that they don't get paid footballers' wages – tend to sigh about such misuse of the language. The manager should have said, 'The boy played brilliantly.' The word 'brilliantly' is an adverb that links with the verb 'played', and, as everyone knows (a phrase that actually means, as only a small number of people know), adverbs usually end in 'ly'. It just sounds wrong when the manager gets it wrong.

The title we have used for this book is 'Write it Right', but it should be 'Write it Correctly' or, even better, 'Write Correctly'. 'Write' is the verb and 'correctly' the adverb. We couldn't call it 'Write it Rightly', as that sounds absurd. So we decided on 'Write it Right', following the same kind of logic that people use when they write or say 'Try it for free', rather than, the more correct, 'Try it for nothing.' That is to say, we opted for the title that is most catchy.

Does it matter that we have produced a book about writing with a slightly suspect title? We would argue that it doesn't. When a football manager makes a mistake in his use of English, it actually adds colour and life to what he is saying; more importantly, we all understand exactly what he means. In the end, this is what matters. This book is about how to write effectively. What matters is whether the reader can understand exactly what the writer was trying to say. The reason we have rules about writing is that the rules help us communicate clearly. But you don't always have to follow the rules to the very last letter. Sometimes, even in the most formal kind of writing exercise, it is a good idea to bend, or break, them.

John Peck and Martin Coyle
Cardiff University

1 The Logic of Effective Writing

▶ **1 The naked truth about writing**

A card in a newsagent's window draws attention to an intriguing offer: 'Alsashun puppies for sale. Going cheep'. Most people reading the card will smile in a slightly superior way. We might not be entirely sure how to spell 'alsatian', but we know that it isn't like the spelling on the card. At the same time, there is something rather endearing about the advertisement, as it is so clear that the person who wrote it ventured forth bravely, trusting that the spelling of the word would echo its sound. But that is not the only spelling mistake. If we did not know better, we might be tempted to take a look at these dogs as they appear to be quite remarkable animals: rather than barking, they do bird impersonations, going 'cheep'.

It is very easy to laugh at such revealing evidence of someone else's educational shortcomings. In a patronising way, we make all kinds of assumptions about the person who wrote this advertisement. There are just six words on the card, but they seem to reveal the naked truth about the owner of the alsatian and its puppies. What is alarming to realise, however, is that all of us reveal the naked truth about ourselves every time another person reads something we have written. For example, you might have to write a letter applying for a job at a local supermarket; the manager, who could well be a university graduate, sees immediately that you are applying for a job, but then proceeds to evaluate you as a person on the basis of the quality of the letter you have written. This happens every time you write, whether it is a letter, a piece of work at school, an essay at university or something as ephemeral as an email to a friend. The person who reads what you have written looks beyond the obvious content and makes an assessment of you. In a way this is terrifying. It means that every piece of writing you produce is a kind of audition. At school, for example, you might dash off a piece of work the night before it is due to be handed in, assuming that nobody is going to pay all that much attention to it. But the teacher reading it is feeding the impression formed from that piece of homework into a more general impression, which will eventually contribute to the reference you receive when you leave school or apply to university.

It makes sense, therefore, to do the best you can in terms of projecting a positive image of yourself every time you write. That, however, is easier said than done. All of us want to convey an impression of ourselves as capable and intelligent, but there are so many things that can go wrong when we write. Time and time again, there is such a gulf between what we were trying to say and what we have actually said. And on top of that there are all those tiny errors in writing, such as commas in the wrong place, and embarrassing spelling mistakes. The worrying possibility is that such mistakes might be revealing the naked truth about our shortcomings. The good news, however, is that most writing difficulties are very superficial and easily dealt with. The problem is that we learnt how to write at primary school, and most of us have never taken a refresher course dealing with the challenges that have to be met in more ambitious forms of writing and in more demanding contexts. This is what this book offers: it is a refresher course on how to sharpen and advance your writing skills (although this will necessarily involve reiterating some of the most basic information about the mechanics of language, especially grammar, punctuation and spelling). At every point in the book, however, we have also kept another idea in mind: as writing always offers a revealing sense of the person behind the words, we consistently try to show how you can project a positive impression of yourself in everything you write.

▶ 2 If you can write an effective letter, you can write anything

Look at the letter below. It is the kind of letter sent and received thousands, possibly millions, of times every day. We have included it here because it provides a neat and simple illustration of the three premises of all effective writing.

This letter relies upon a method that is very widely used for routine business correspondence. Every paragraph is a new sentence that conveys just one fact in the simplest and most direct terms. The reason why businesses and other organisations adopt this method is that it makes for a very clear letter, reducing the possibility of ambiguous or confusing statements. The writer simply works through the sequence of steps, with a fresh sentence in the letter for every action taken. If, when the letter is written, anything strikes the writer as being unclear,

Gap Year Projects
4 Barchester Mews
Barchester
BR16 4GR

0771 222 5566

Mr Robert Ross
35 Middle Street
Middlemarch
MD4 5TH

23 November 2007

Dear Robert

Thank you for submitting your application form to Gap Year Projects.

I am pleased to inform you that, on the basis of the information provided, we are recommending that you can advance to the next stage for a position on one of our projects in South America.

We will contact you again within a fortnight in order to arrange an interview.

If that interview is successful, we will require an immediate payment of £500 as your initial contribution to the cost of the placement.

In the meantime, if you have any questions, do not hesitate to contact me.

Yours sincerely

Sophie Wait
Overseas Projects Coordinator

he or she can incorporate additional one-sentence paragraphs or tinker with the expression of the separate sentences.

It is, of course, the case that the 'one paragraph = one sentence' approach is not going to prove appropriate in all forms of writing. Indeed, a job application that consisted of 50 or more separate paragraphs would look silly. But the idea of working through what one has to say in a logical and orderly sequence, the steps in the sequence being made clear by the division into paragraphs, is one of the fundamental secrets of good writing. There are two other secrets. The first, which comes before anything else, is grasping the conventions of the writing exercise you are engaged upon. The conventions that determine the shape of this letter are very straightforward; when it comes to writing an essay, the shaping conventions might be rather more complicated, but a lot of the difficult work on an essay is done in advance if you can recognise the nature of the conventions involved. Perhaps the major secret of writing, however, is saying what one has to say in sentences that are as simple and as straightforward as possible. We deal with the importance of recognising the conventions you are working with, establishing a logical and orderly sequence for your writing, and writing in simple sentences, in the next three units.

▶ 3 Familiarise yourself with, and employ the standard conventions of, the writing exercise you are undertaking

Whatever kind of writing you embark upon, there will be conventions associated with that form of writing which you must follow. The onus is upon you as a student to make yourself aware of, and conform to, the conventions in force. Why? Well, there is one very good reason. Clever students will make sure that they know and use the conventions. Some other students, by contrast, will never really realise that a set of conventions exists. These will be the students who then go on to show signs of weakness in every aspect of their written work. Another reason for having conventions in any form of writing, however, is that they help you organise what you have to say, and they also help the person who is reading what you have written. In other words, they help you communicate. Later in this book, we will turn to the conventions of essay writing, but for the moment we want to concentrate on letter writing.

This is a genuine letter sent by a university student (although we have changed his name); this is all he wrote and everything he wrote. His failure to observe the basic conventions not only creates a poor impression but also renders the letter essentially meaningless:

Dear Sir
I have been off college for two weeks with a serious chest infection. I would like it if you could take into account my absence from this part of the course when assessing my work for this term.
Yours sincerely

J. Smith

Not many letters from students will be as shoddy as this, but many people do miss out some or all of the things that this student has missed out. The student has not provided his address. As there is more than one person called J. Smith taking the course, we cannot be sure, therefore, who the student is. There is no date on the letter. Consequently, we do not know what period the student is referring to when he mentions that he has been ill. The letter is also abrupt to the point of rudeness (there is a major issue involved here, which we return to again and again in the second half of this book, which is achieving the right tone in writing). In his defence the student would probably say that this is just a note that he dashed off quickly. But if most of the students in a class are making an effort to do more than just dash off a note quickly, the careless student is bound to miss out in the end.

What makes his slackness more obvious is that the conventions of letter writing are so simple and so easy to master. This is the basic pattern and layout of any formal or business letter (if you are writing a personal letter, for example a love letter, you can make up your own conventions):

	Address
	Telephone number
Name and address of recipient	
Date	
Reference number (if appropriate)	
Salutation	
	Subject matter (sometimes)
Paragraph 1	
Paragraph 2	
Paragraph 3	
Conclusion	
Signature	

You must start with your address. Conventions about small details change over the years. There was a time, for example, when you were expected to include a comma between the house number and street name, a comma at the end of each line, and a full stop at the end of the address, but the advent of word-processors and quality printers has made those conventions appear fussy and superfluous. There was a time, too, when you were supposed to include the county name in an address, but the Post Office changed this convention a few years ago; the town and postcode (zip code) together tell us all we need to know. When you include a number after the address, you do not need to write 'Telephone' beforehand; it is, after all, pretty obvious that this is your telephone number and not a set of lottery numbers.

You then move on to the name and address of the person you are writing to (although you would not bother to include this in personal letters), and the date. Once upon a time people would write '29th June, 2007', but these days the punctuation seems superfluous. You could, therefore, write '29th June 2007' or '29 June 2007' (or, in the USA, June 29, 2007). If you are replying to a business letter that included a reference number it is helpful to mention that reference number in your letter, below the name and address of the recipient. You then move on to the salutation. There used to be lots of variants of this, but these days it is 'Dear Sir', or 'Dear Madam', or 'Dear Sir/Madam' if you are at all unsure of the gender of the recipient, or 'Dear Mr Jones', or whoever, if you know the name of the recipient. If the letter starts with 'Dear Sir' or 'Dear Madam', you sign off with 'Yours faithfully'. If you start with the person's name, you sign off with 'Yours sincerely'. There is no choice involved here; this distinction is absolute, and is one of the key signals to your reader that you have taken care over the letter. A semi-formal letter, for example a letter between two colleagues at work, might end with 'Yours truly', but otherwise it is always 'Yours faithfully' or 'Yours sincerely' (and note that it is a lower case 'f' and a lower case 's').

The body of the letter might mention the subject matter if you feel that helps. For example, if you had written to an airline, and if your letter was headed 'Claim for Lost Baggage', that might speed up your letter's arrival in the right department. In our outline of a letter, above, we have listed 'Paragraph' three times; as will be discussed in the next unit, three paragraphs is nearly always the best way to organise a letter. It is a convention of letter writing not to indent at the start of a paragraph; leaving a line of space between paragraphs indicates the start of a new paragraph. You then sign your letter, and that could be it. Increasingly, however, people want to add their email address; it looks too cluttered if you add it at the top, so most people include it after their name (although this convention might well change).

If all that has been too much to take in, you will not go far wrong if you follow the pattern of this letter:

95 Richmond Avenue
Newtown
KF1 4RT

021 2345 6789

Dr Kate Davies
English Literature
Newtown University
PO Box 34
Newtown
KF1 3XB

28th March 2007

Dear Kate

I am writing to apologise for my absence from last week's tutorial.

Unfortunately, on my way to college that morning I was involved in a road accident and, as a result, had to spend the night in hospital for observation. I enclose a copy of a letter from the doctor who attended me.

I am glad to say that I have fully recovered, and that I am now attending college again on a regular basis. I have obtained a photocopy of the handout for next week's class and will see you next Thursday.

Yours sincerely

Charlotte Butler

Charlieb@hotmail.com

▶ 4 Establish a logical and orderly sequence in what you write

The body of the letter at the end of the last unit consisted of three paragraphs. You might feel that all the information could have been conveyed in just one paragraph. Alternatively, the student could have used the business method of a new paragraph for each new point in the letter. But there is a great deal to be said for organising a letter in three paragraphs. In some way it appears to add authority to what you have to say; a letter in three paragraphs sounds convincing and substantial, possibly because it is organised in substantial steps. Or it might be because it resembles the structure of a story, with a beginning, middle and end. As this book goes on, one of the main things we will be suggesting is that any piece of written work is going to be most effective if it is organised in three clear steps. A job or university application, for example, might be organised in three paragraphs, while an essay could move through three very clearly defined stages.

For the moment, however, we want to stick with the idea of a three-paragraph letter. A letter organised in this way follows a logical and orderly sequence. This is what you are likely to be focusing on at each step:

(1) why you are writing
(ii) the fresh information you have to communicate in this letter
(iii) where this gets you and the person you are writing to and/or what the next step or course of action might be.

In the example above, Charlotte writes because she has missed a class, she communicates the circumstances that explain her absence and then, in the third paragraph, she moves on to her state of health and the fact that she will be present next week.

Although dealing with a very different subject matter, this sales letter promoting a new magazine is organised along similar lines. The editor explains why he is writing, makes an offer and then tells the recipient what to do next (as you can see, we have missed out the address etc. and only reproduced the body of the letter).

In today's fast-moving club scene, it's essential that you keep up-to-date with the most important news and all the new music. But getting the right information can be difficult; there's just too much to listen to and too much to take in. Fortunately there's an answer at hand. It's called KLUBB and it's a NEW magazine that distils what you really need to know.

But here's the best news of all. This is your opportunity to try KLUBB risk-free with six FREE issues. There's absolutely no obligation and nothing to pay. That's right, there's absolutely NO catch, so please don't send any money with your order. The SIX issues I'll send you are FREE with my compliments.

Claiming your SIX FREE issues couldn't be easier. Simply tick the box on the order form and return it in the postage paid envelope provided. If you agree that KLUBB is a magazine you can't afford to be without, you will – after you have received your SIX FREE issues – be given the opportunity to join us as a subscriber. But that is for you to decide. Your SIX FREE issues will be sent totally without obligation.

This might not be the style that you would adopt if you were writing to your bank manager ('In today's fast-spending student culture, this is your opportunity to give me an INTEREST-FREE overdraft immediately, and totally without ANY OBLIGATION on my part' would not go down very well), but the repetition and emphasis serve a purpose here. The main reason why the letter is effective, however, is because of the logical way in which it is organised in three paragraphs. Whatever the subject matter of your letter, 99 times out a 100 it should be possible to organise what you have to say in a letter in three distinct paragraph steps. You might, if you don't believe us, start by taking a critical look at the letters you receive. You will probably find that the vast majority, and certainly the ones you judge as clear and effective, are structured in three paragraphs.

How to establish a logical and orderly sequence in a letter

1. Think in three steps:

   (i)   why you are writing
   (ii) the fresh information you have to communicate in this letter
   (iii) where this gets you and the person you are writing to and/or what the next step or course of action might be.

2. Use a separate paragraph for each of these steps in your letter.

3. If the body of the letter consists of more than three paragraphs, think about whether the letter could be better organised as three paragraphs.

▶ 5 Control the length of sentences

Let us imagine that you are writing something – not necessarily a letter. You have followed the standard conventions, and you are also reasonably happy that what you have written reflects a logical and orderly sequence of thought (in other words, that there is a beginning, a middle and an end to what you have written). But what most people worry about is that their individual sentences will let them down: that the sentences don't really say what they want them to say, and that the sentences might not be correctly punctuated or grammatical. We cannot deal with all the issues involved here (these are discussed in later sections), but we can deal with the principal secret of how to write mechanically correct sentences. The answer is, 'keep it simple'.

Here is a letter that an insurance assessor sent to a builder about a claim. The builder interpreted the letter as meaning that the claim was being refused, but when he phoned the assessor it turned out that the claim was being allowed, with just one small deduction for the repair to a length of copper pipe. But this is not at all clear in the letter. How does the writer manage to get in such a tangle?

> I write, in reference to the above incident, and to advise that I am in receipt of your estimates for the reinstatement due to water damage.
>
> The estimates are acceptable however in connection with the dismantling of the fitted cabinets in order to remove the section of copper pipe. It is apparent that the Insured's policy will not cover the repair to the pipe work.
>
> Therefore can you please confirm in writing the total cost for the repair to the pipe work in order to deduct from your estimate of £560.

As you can see, it is the middle paragraph that really fails to make sense, although the last paragraph also has problems. What is going wrong is that the assessor is thinking out loud. He could convey his meaning if he were speaking the same words, because pauses and changes of emphasis would make the meaning clear. But in writing, the meaning can only be signalled by punctuation.

What poor writers tend to do is to merge one sentence (and one idea) into the next sentence (and next idea). The meaning then becomes obscured. It might surprise you to hear that in GCSE English examinations it is the weakest candidates who write the longest sentences; essentially, they just string lots of words together. What they are trying to say creates little impact and often fails to make sense. It is, of course, the case that good writers also use long sentences, but they tend to enlarge their sentences by incorporating additional clauses along the way. A weak writer states one idea and then tries to stick another one on without realising that it would make more sense to start a fresh sentence. It is often the case that an awkward phrase – in the first paragraph of this letter, 'to advise that' – has to be called upon to make the link between the two ideas. The remedy is to keep the sentences as brief and direct as possible.

This letter could be rewritten as follows.

> I write in reference to the above incident. I am in receipt of your estimates for the reinstatement due to water damage.
>
> The estimates are acceptable. However, in connection with the dismantling of the fitted cabinets in order to remove the section of copper pipe, the policy does not cover the repair to the pipe work.
>
> Therefore, can you please confirm in writing the total cost for the repair to the pipe work? This will be deducted from your estimate of £560.

The original letter has been broken down into smaller sentences, although in the middle paragraph there is still a rather awkward second sentence with an unwieldy subordinate clause. Even that could be changed very simply:

> The estimates are acceptable. However, the policy does not cover the repair to the pipe work in the fitted cabinets nor the dismantling of them.

The lesson that can be drawn from this example can be applied to all forms of writing. Sentences should be short and to the point, unless you have something really complex to say. It is, even then, often the case that a complex idea can be conveyed most clearly if you break it down into a number of separate sentences. The way to check what you have written is to read it out loud to yourself. If it sounds awkward, if

---

How to control the length of sentences

1. Your controlling principle should be that one idea equals one sentence.

2. Remember that the next idea demands a fresh sentence.

3. Do not run sentences into each other. You might need to incorporate subordinate clauses (that is, additional information within the body of the sentence), but that is not the same as stringing sentences together.

4. Read what you have written out loud to yourself. Have you relied upon awkward phrases to get from one point to the next? If you have, the phrase can probably be cut and a fresh sentence started.

it fails to make sense, or if you run out of breath in reading the sentence, then the sentence is probably too long. If cumbersome phrases, such as *to advise that*, pop up in the middle of a sentence, then you are probably desperately trying to link two separate sentences together.

▶ 6 Always check your English, and always be prepared to rewrite

Most letters will not involve mistakes as extreme as those in the example above. It is the case, however, that many pieces of writing, ranging from letters to essays, are littered with tiny mistakes that undermine the credibility of the writer. Here, for example, is part of a letter written by a sixth-former applying for a university scholarship.

> I enjoy reading a wide range of literary texts especially novels written by the Brontës, and contemporary women writers. Having read most of the Brontë works my favourite is *Wuthering Heights*. I particularly like the way Emily Brontë portrays the character of Heathcliffe, as a romantic hero but also a melancholy and brutal person. *Wuthering Heights* is, in my opinion a novel of timeless romance.

The name of the character the student refers to is Heathcliff, not Heathcliffe. We might well ask, if she loves this book so much, how come she failed to notice the correct spelling of the hero's name? This is, however, typical of the kind of small but embarrassing mistakes that people make in writing. What is the answer? Well, we might say, don't make the mistake in the first place. But when you have written something, you need to check what you have written very carefully. If what you have written is something important or something that is going to be read by a number of people, it also makes sense to get someone else to check it.

What you must also tell yourself is that when you have finished writing something, that is not the end of the process. What you have written is merely the first draft. You must be prepared to check and polish your work. These days, when so much is written on word-processors, this is a great deal easier to do than at any time in the past. But because it is so easy to do, expectations are higher. Thirty years ago people might have turned a blind eye to small failings in a piece of writing, but today, in a nicely printed letter, mistakes leap out.

Apart from the wrong spelling of Heathcliff's name, this letter is also characterised by some oddly misplaced commas. This is a shortcoming that is commonplace. But how is it possible to avoid committing such errors? It is all very well for someone to tell you to check what you have written, but that does not help all that much if you do not know the rules. Reading what you have written out loud to yourself might help you identify where the pauses, and therefore the commas, should be. And every sensible person will get someone else to check what they have written. But what if your friends and family know even less than you about the positioning of commas?

The only real advice we can offer is to read very closely the section on commas in this book. The logic of commas is really easy – it is just like changing gear when driving – and it is possible to improve one's command of commas in a day. If you do not control your punctuation, you obscure the meaning of what you are trying to say.

These are the minor adjustments the student needed to make:

> I enjoy reading a wide range of literary texts, especially novels written by the Brontës and contemporary women writers. Having read most of the Brontë works, my favourite is *Wuthering Heights*. I particularly like the way Emily Brontë portrays the character of Heathcliff, not only as a romantic hero but also as a melancholy and brutal person. *Wuthering Heights* is, in my opinion, a novel of timeless romance.

This is not the point at which to explain why we have made the alterations we have made. The principles involved are explained later in this book. But you might try reading out loud the two versions of this letter, which might suggest something about the logic of the comma. A comma always indicates a momentary pause in the advance or movement of a sentence; this can be appreciated when a sentence is read out loud, but it is also the case that reading a sentence out loud can indicate where commas need to be inserted.

▶ 7 When you write anything, think hard about the impression you are creating

This is a letter from someone applying for a university place. The applicant, before applying a second time through the Universities and Colleges Admissions Service (UCAS), decided to write directly to a number of departments. If you were the tutor in charge of admissions, would you offer this candidate a place?

Dear Sir Madam,

I have now just completed my A-level exams and have now completed my time at school. I will be taking a gap year before hopefully going to university. However as yet I have no places. The reason being that I applied last year to study Geography. But after much deliberation with my parent's I concluded that I acted too hastily in my application's. Therefore I decided to decline any offers and to give myself more time to consider the vast array of options open to me.

After a lot of research I have decided to study History at degree level. I was just wondering if under my irregular situation I would be considered equally with other applicants if I were to apply to your department to study History. Or if my situation would count against me. Or render me at a disadvantage. Also what grades would allow me to apply to your department to study History with any success.

I would be ever so grateful if you could answer my question's and cast a light upon my situation, so I thank you for your time.

Yours Sincerly

Andrew Grant

Do you suspect that his earlier applications might well have failed to result in any offers? Could this have been because the Personal Statement on his previous application was characterised by the kind of errors in English that are evident here?

It is probably the case that you can see there are problems with the English in this letter, but would find it hard to identify precisely what the mistakes are. In a moment we will touch on how and why things are going wrong, but first we want to stress that this is very close to being an extremely effective letter. The applicant (we have changed his name) is certainly not lacking in ability. It is just that he has been careless, devoting too little thought to the impression he is creating. Most of us can remember how carefully we drove during our driving test, whereas in our day-to-day driving we now pay far less attention to the rules. In writing (unless it is sending an email to a friend) you always have to obey the rules.

The main problem with this letter is that the applicant has simply dashed off his thoughts. There is a sound basic structure to his letter, which moves very clearly through three paragraphs, but there are sentences that need polishing and editing, sentences that are not actually sentences, redundant words and phrases, and something a touch wrong and awkward about the tone. We are not going to examine and explain the mistakes in detail here. But because this letter is so representative of how students write when they do not take enough care, we want to offer an amended version of the letter to indicate just how little corrective surgery is required. The letter as it stands creates a poor impression. If the student had gone through the letter carefully, reading it out loud and thinking about whether things sounded right, the chances are that most of the shortcomings could have been eliminated.

Dear Sir/Madam

I have just completed my A-level exams and have, therefore, now completed my time at school. I will be taking a gap year before going to university. At the moment, however, I do not have a place. I applied to study Geography, but after much deliberation I concluded that I acted too hastily in my choice of subject.

I have now decided that I wish to study History at degree level. Given my irregular situation, would I be considered equally with other applicants if I were to apply to your department? In particular, would my previous application to study Geography render me at a disadvantage? It would also be very helpful if you could tell me what grades would enable me to apply to your department with any hope of success.

I would be very grateful for any help and clarification you can offer.

Yours faithfully

Andrew Grant

Perhaps the most significant change we have made is that we have cut back a verbose letter. Inevitably, cutting away the dead wood has added to the sharpness of definition of what remains. The chances are that just about everything you write – that is, anything from a letter to an essay – could be pruned, trimmed and made stronger in this kind of way.

▶ 8 I only want to write something! You make it sound as if there are about a million rules that have to be mastered first

Having read this far in this book, you might well decide that you will not bother to write any letters in future, that it is easier to phone. But there are times when you have to put things in writing, and these could be the most important times, such as when you are applying for a job or a university place, defending your actions in a letter to a magistrate, making an insurance claim or asking someone for help or money. In such circumstances you always need to present yourself in the best possible light.

The other point we must make is that, whatever this section might have implied, writing a letter – indeed, writing anything – is not rocket science. All that is required is a degree of care. When it comes to letter writing, there are six main points to bear in mind. You might not bother with all of these at all times, but you must do so if your letter matters:

1   Familiarise yourself with and employ the standard conventions of letter writing.
2   If you are replying to a letter that strikes you as clear and competent, use the letter you have received as a model for the format of your own letter.
3   Try to establish a logical and orderly sequence (why you are writing, the fresh information you have to communicate in this letter, where this gets you and the person you are writing to and/or what the next step might be).
4   Use separate paragraphs for the different logical steps in your letter.
5   Control the length of your sentences.
6   If this is anything other than a personal letter, regard what you have written so far as a first draft. Check your English, and be prepared to rewrite sentences in your letter. Read your draft out loud to yourself. As far as you can, check your English. Then get someone else to check your letter and English.

More briefly, follow the conventions, pay attention to the overall pattern and structure of what you are writing, and pay attention to the details of what you are writing. As we explain in the next unit, the same principles govern all forms of writing.

▶ 9 How do these guidelines about letter writing relate to other forms of writing?

Proficiency in letter writing relates in a very direct way to proficiency in all forms of writing. In essence, the skills required in letter writing are the same skills that are called upon in producing all written work. The essential steps can be summarised very briefly.

How the guidelines that apply in letter writing relate to other forms of writing

1. All forms of writing have their own conventions. Make sure you have grasped the conventions of the writing exercise you have embarked upon.

2. If you are replying to a letter, the letter you have received will often provide a model that you can follow. In all forms of writing, it is usually possible to find a model that will provide you with an idea of the conventions to employ.

3. Try to grasp the importance of a logical and orderly sequence in any piece of writing.

4. Try to grasp the logic of thinking and writing in clear paragraph steps.

5. Appreciate just how much it is possible to say in simple and straightforward sentences. Remember that intelligent students tend to write shorter sentences than less able students.

6. Accept that it is the final polish – working on the draft version until it is a version you can feel proud of – that makes all the difference in the world. At university, for example, the difference between the student who gets a lower second degree and the student who gets an upper second is usually as simple as the fact that the better student took a little extra time revising and polishing every piece of written work along the way.

▶ **10 Do the conventions and rules about letter writing apply to emails?**

We have probably reached a point where more emails than letters are sent every day. Emails have their own conventions, which might be summed up quickly by saying that the old conventions do not apply any more. For example, if you are sending the equivalent of a letter as an email, you do not include your address, the name and address of your recipient or the date, simply because the computer will have generated all this information. Generally speaking, most people in an email do not start with the salutation 'Dear'. And most people don't bother with 'Yours faithfully' or 'Yours sincerely'. All of this might seem like a case of getting rid of redundant conventions, but in fact it is just a case of replacing one set of conventions with a new set designed to indicate that the medium of electronic mail is immediate and urgent. The implicit message is that writing letters is too slow; this is a message that must be transmitted as quickly as possible.

This is borne out in another feature of emails: indifference about 'correct' English. Lots of people don't bother with capital letters when writing an email; one American academic told us that he didn't have enough time in his working life to mess around shifting to CAPS on his keyboard. Similarly, if you make a spelling mistake in writing an email, the convention is that you do not bother to correct it. The recipient will assume that it was a typing error, rather than ignorance. And sentences in an email can be as long, as ungrammatical and as ambiguous as you wish without anyone really condemning you. The assumption is that you dashed off what you had to say at speed because life today is too hectic to dawdle over the traditional literary virtues.

We go along with all of this entirely. Most of the emails we write dozens of times a day include sentences such as 'Thnak yuo for the infromation. Ill pass it on to Rihcard immdeiately.' There comes a point, however, where the emails you send are too important to be sent in an unrevised state. There is just one question you have to ask: will someone be judging me on the basis of what I have written? If you were a solicitor, for example, and sent a garbled and rather confusing email, it could jeopardise the case you were working on. The conse-quences could be extremely serious. In a not dissimilar way, if you were making a late 'Clearing' application to a university and contacted an admissions tutor, a poorly written email could create the impression that you were not good enough to be offered a place. And supposing you were applying, via email, for a job, something that is now very common. In any kind of job application, the letter of application is the first stage of the interview. A great many things about your suitability for the post are decided on the basis of not just the content of your application but also the literacy of your application.

The lesson, therefore, is the same lesson as with letter writing. If the email does not really matter – for example, if you are sending a message to a friend who is three feet away from you sitting at the next computer in a university library – you do not have to take care. But if it matters – which means, if you are writing something that creates an impression of you in a context that matters – then you must take care. In the case of an email, that means ensuring that the email is logical and structured, and that you feel happy with the quality of each individual sentence. Redrafting might go against the grain of communication by email, but it is essential whenever you judge attention to detail to be in your interest.

2 Applying for a Course, Applying for a Job

▶ 11 I would like to make a personal statement (and I would like someone to read it)

'My passion for English Literature . . . '. An application for a university place, and yet another in which the applicant starts their personal statement with a declaration of their passion for the subject. The admissions tutor groans. And it happens in every subject: 'My passion for Civil Engineering . . . ', 'My passion for Law . . . ', 'My passion for Accountancy . . . '. Here we go again with the same well-worn words.

It will probably surprise you to hear that a lot of university admissions tutors don't read the personal statements on university application forms. Or, more precisely, they don't read them in the kind of way you would expect. You might assume that they will be interested in your declaration of your passion for the subject and the information about just how busy you have been both inside and outside school. And to a certain extent they are. But admissions tutors don't just look at the content of a personal statement. What they focus on is the form of the personal statement. Does the applicant show good judgement in knowing how much or how little to write, and what to include and exclude? And does the applicant show an ability to think logically? This will be apparent if the statement is written in a structured and organised manner. If applicants are unable to make such judgements in putting together their applications, they are likely to betray a similar lack of judgement in their written work at university.

There is, in addition, one other thing that admissions tutors always take a great deal of notice of. Does the student know how to spell and punctuate? This is very important. You would be amazed just how many applicants talk about their desire to '*persue' a subject, when the correct spelling is 'pursue', and how many applicants talk about their '*sucesses' at school, whereas we would far rather hear about their 'successes'. Spelling and punctuation errors are extraordinarily revealing. Of course, everybody makes slips, and no one expects you to know everything when you are still at school. What is more worrying is that spelling and punctuation errors reveal a failure to take care: after all, you are filling in just one form. No department really wants to offer places to applicants who cannot be bothered to check what they have written.

This section of the book is mainly about constructing a personal statement for a university application, but everything we say – about how to structure your statement, about how much or how little information to include, and about the need to pay attention to how you express yourself – holds true in respect of whatever you are applying for, be it a course or a job, and at every level, right through from school until when you are well established in a career. A student told us the other day about how humiliated she felt in her interview for a teachers' training course when they asked why there were three spelling mistakes in her application. If it is an academic course you are applying for, your personal statement must demonstrate your academic competence. And getting it right is going to be even more important when it comes to a job application, as there could be dozens, possibly even hundreds, of people applying for one job. Presumably the semi-literate applications go straight in the bin, with no chance of an interview. But so will the applications that don't command the employer's attention. Whatever you are applying for, you must ensure that you put together a professional and persuasive impression of who you are.

▶ 12 How do you sell yourself?

Where all this leads is that you have got to think very carefully about how you present, even sell, yourself in your personal statement. In meeting this challenge, it is your ability as a writer that is of first importance. Nobody, however, is born with knowledge about how to write. There might be a few people who instinctively can write a confident character sketch of themselves, but most people will need help and guidance. The following units are about the strategies involved in projecting a good impression of yourself.

The first point to grasp is that the same strategies are equally valid in all forms of writing. The principles we established in the last section, therefore, the principles that apply in letter writing, can also be called upon when writing an application for a place at university or for a job. You have to start by recognising the conventions of the writing exercise. You then have to organise your work in a structured and logical way, making sure that you write in clear and correct English. And, finally, you have to polish and perfect – in other words, draft and redraft – every detail of what you have written.

We'll begin with the conventions of writing a personal statement. There might not appear to be clear conventions in the same kind of way there are in letter writing, but certain things are understood. For a start, you only have a limited amount of space at your disposal. Far too many people try to cram as much information and as many words as they can into this space. Remind yourself that conventions in writing are there to help you as the writer, but also there to help your reader understand with a minimum of effort what you have written. An admissions tutor doesn't want to be confronted by a great wodge of words in the tiniest typeface imaginable. This, of course, also applies to the references for students supplied by schools and colleges; teachers writing references can be just as long-winded as their pupils. The admissions tutor wants to be able to see and take in almost immediately what you (and then the person writing your reference) have to say.

The basic convention of writing your personal statement, therefore, is that, rather like a guest who is displaying good manners, you introduce yourself politely, saying what you have to say but not boring your host by going on for too long. In just about every form of writing there is no more useful maxim than 'less is more', and it certainly applies when writing a personal statement. In turn, this starts to involve some very careful judgements about what to include and what to miss out, and how to construct an economical, yet telling, account of yourself. It is how these decisions reflect themselves in the quality of what you write that is all-important. The admissions tutor, you can be sure, is looking at the skill with which you have constructed your economical yet powerful sales pitch.

There are two ways of writing anything. Some people just start writing, going on until they have said everything they want to say. Other people plan and prepare what they are going to say in advance before putting pen to paper. Generally speaking, the second method always produces a stronger result. When you set about writing a personal statement, it makes a lot of sense to think in terms of three paragraphs. In the first paragraph you need to introduce yourself, in the second you might add important or additional information that has not been conveyed in the first paragraph, and in your final paragraph you could change tack slightly, writing about yourself from a different angle (for example, dwelling on your social interests as opposed to your academic record). This kind of three-paragraph package presents your reader with a coherent and easy to digest impression. To add to the impression of coherence and organisation in your writing, it makes sense to think about having three clusters of sentences (or possibly just three sentences) in each paragraph. That will ensure that, rather than trailing on, your statement will consistently be adding new material in a tightly controlled and easily absorbed fashion. Finally, you must turn your attention to polishing and tightening the expression of what you have written.

How to write a personal statement

1. Establish the conventions of this particular writing exercise.

2. Organise a structured and economical account of yourself.

3. Write in clear, straightforward and correct English.

4. Make sure that each paragraph is tightly structured, and that you have checked and polished what you have written.

► 13 There is no excuse for carelessness

None of this advice will mean all that much until we start to consider some examples of impressive and unimpressive personal statements. Let's start with the first paragraph from one applicant.

I have always expressed a keen love of English literature; which is my favourite pass-time. I especially like close reading of the texts analysing how the authors use the language and the imagery to capture a specific mood or tone, and developing a personal response. I enjoy it thoroughly. I enjoy writing as well as reading. I am a senior prefect in my school. I would consider English teaching at some point in the future. To this end I took work experience in a local primary school, and found it fairly rewarding.

The trouble with this is that it reads like a first draft. The applicant has noted down a few stray thoughts, but has then failed to move on to the stage of organising and revising what she has written.

But, rather than criticising what she has written in general terms, we need to ask what are the specific faults with the application. First, she hasn't really grasped the conventions of this form of writing, or, in other words, the nature of the exercise. Look at how the sentences nearly all start with the word 'I'. It is as if she believes that the personal statement is, quite literally, a 'personal' statement, in the sense of being a chance to talk about herself in a rather self-indulgent way. It hasn't struck her that she should be paying just as much attention to the form of what she is writing as she does to the content. At the moment this sounds rather more like the student chatting than writing. The lack of thought about the impact of what she has said also reveals itself in the lack of any purposeful shape to the paragraph. A paragraph, essentially, should develop one idea or theme; it needs to have a feeling of self-sufficient coherence, before the next paragraph moves on to the next idea or theme. But this applicant strays from her love of English to work experience, informing us along the way, in a sentence that does not connect with anything else being said, that she is a senior prefect.

The failure to structure and organise the paragraph is matched by careless mistakes in just about every sentence. It is very clear that the applicant has not read this out loud to herself. The two most embarrassing mistakes in her use of English are of the kind that students make over and over again. She should have asked herself if she was using the right words, and whether she was spelling the words correctly. It is often the case that students, trying to impress, use a long word when a short word would work better; more often than not, the long word will be the wrong word. At the start the applicant is saying 'I have always had a keen love of English literature.' It doesn't really make sense to say that she has 'expressed' a love of the subject. '*Pass-time' is not a word; what she means is 'pastime'. And if she had read her statement out loud, she would probably have spotted that 'the language and the imagery' sounds wrong, that what she is trying to say is how authors use 'language and imagery'. With regard to punctuation, the first sentence requires a comma rather than a semicolon, as 'which is my favourite subject' is a subordinate clause relating to English literature.

Finally, and this is an important point that is all too often overlooked, it is necessary to think about the tone of what you have written. Does it seem to strike the right note? In this application, surely there is something just a little bit wrong about 'found it fairly rewarding'. It is grudging. It doesn't establish the right kind of positive attitude. The criticisms we have offered here might seem damning, but, in fact, the mistakes this candidate has made are common in all forms of writing: a failure to judge the nature of the exercise, lack of structure, careless mistakes and a failure to re-read what has been written to see whether it strikes the right note throughout. The applicant, in a sense, isn't writing all that badly, just writing in the way that a great many people do a great deal of the time.

▶ 14 The importance of structure

Here is another personal statement taken from a university application. This time, however, for reasons that will become clear, we have reproduced the entire statement. This is better written than the previous example, but there are some very simple ways in which it could be improved in order to create more of an impact.

Having enjoyed reading throughout my school life, I have always taken it for granted that I would study English at university. It is a subject I both like and excel in. I read avidly, and am particularly fond of nineteenth-century fiction; in the sixth-form, in addition to set texts, I have read most of Austen and Hardy, and also novels by Dickens and Eliot.

Although it could be maintained that close analysis of a text causes it to lose its 'magic', I have found to the contrary that many texts cannot be fully appreciated without the fuller understanding to which this study leads.

I am a regular member of our School Literary Society, where we express our views on literature and current affairs and hear a range of outside speakers. This has enabled me, together with my participation in the School Debating Society, to extend my communication skills by discussing a variety of skills other than in a classroom situation.

I have an eclectic taste in music and have been involved in a variety of musical events. I am a member of the school orchestra and have been centrally involved in starting a school jazz band. I perform in school concerts and productions, and have travelled in Holland, Belgium and Spain musically. I relish opportunities to play the violin, harp and piano.

After my degree course, I hope to further my education to become a primary school teacher. I have completed work experience in both a local primary school and nursery.

Within school I have taken joint responsibility for a Year Seven group, which entails ensuring that the younger students settle comfortably into their new environment and introducing them to a variety of extra-curricular activities our school offers. I have also assisted teachers in lower school lessons.

> During the Sixth Form I have found my studies very rewarding. I find that the study of grammar in French helps me to understand the use of grammar in English constructions. In my studies of Classical Civilisation I am particularly interested in the works of Homer, as The Odyssey is widely acclaimed as the model of so much later literature.
>
> Outside school I have taken on weekend work as a supplement to my income, which has been a valuable experience.
>
> I look forward to studying English at a higher level and continuing to use the skills I have learnt to help others to appreciate it as I do.

Let's start with a little stylistic trick. It usually makes sense in writing to start with a bold and simple opening sentence; it is nearly always a mistake to open with a sentence that begins with a subsidiary clause. Here, rather than writing 'Having enjoyed reading throughout my school life . . . ', it would have been a good move in editing the statement to start with 'I have always taken it for granted that I would study English at university'. It might seem a trivial change, but it is such trivial changes that make the difference between merely ordinary and really effective writing.

That, however, is a minor quibble about an extremely good personal statement. This is a good candidate. The admissions tutor is likely to take account of the content of this application, in part because the applicant, rather than making vague gestures, provides a lot of concrete detail about what she has read and what she has been doing. But this only works because the sentences are, for the most part, literate and well written. Clearly and helpfully, they draw attention to the content without the admissions tutor having to decode or correct the English in order to get at what the applicant is saying. So, where is the problem?

The only real weakness is that the account straggles through too many paragraphs; by the end, with nine paragraphs, the statement strikes the reader as rambling rather than as coherent and well organised. It would work a lot better if it were to be reorganised into three paragraphs. The candidate could focus on her enjoyment of English, her other interests, and her plans for the future. Some of the paragraphs can be ditched, as they tend to weaken rather than enhance the overall impression. What we might add is that sometimes the applicant is trying too hard in her sentences; they can, therefore, afford to lose a few words along the way. And also, in the process of reading sentences out loud to see if they sound right, we have made quite a few tiny alterations in order and expression:

I have always taken it for granted that I would study English at university. It is a subject I both like and excel in. I read avidly, and am particularly fond of nineteenth-century fiction; in the sixth-form, in addition to set texts, I have read most of Austen and Hardy, and also novels by Dickens and Eliot. Although it could be maintained that close analysis of a text causes it to lose its 'magic', I have found, to the contrary, that many texts cannot be fully appreciated without the fuller understanding that this kind of study brings.

I am a regular member of our School Literary Society, where we express our views on literature and current affairs and hear a range of outside speakers. This has enabled me, together with my participation in the School Debating Society, to extend my communication skills. My main recreational interest is music; I play the violin, harp and piano, and have been involved in a wide variety of musical events. I am a member of the school orchestra and have been centrally involved in starting a school jazz band. I perform in school concerts and productions, and have participated in school music tours of Holland, Belgium and Spain.

After my degree course, I hope to become a primary school teacher. I have completed work experience in a local primary school and a local nursery. Within school, I have taken joint responsibility for a Year Seven group, which involves ensuring that younger pupils settle comfortably into their new environment and encouraging them to take part in a variety of extra-curricular activities. I have also assisted teachers in lower school lessons. I look forward to studying English at a higher level, and then, as a teacher, helping others to appreciate the subject as I do.

If this strikes you as an improvement on the original, note the three steps we have taken. First, recognising the conventions of this writing exercise, we determined a clear subject focus for each paragraph. We then tinkered with the original to produce a tight and economical account in each paragraph. And then finally, and perhaps most importantly, we tinkered with the sentences, losing words if possible, until everything struck us as on target. This kind of polishing, especially on a matter as important as a university application form, might be something that you have to return to intermittently over the course of several days. What helps immediately, however, is presenting your writing in three paragraph blocks. The original version was almost unreadable, crowding too much material into a small space. This is a common fault seen on many university application forms, and in every other kind of course or job application: candidates feel they must put down as much as possible, and so pay too little attention to the impact this has on the reader. A well-structured, clear frame will allow you to say everything you have to say in a much more effective, thoughtful way.

▶ 15 'Too much gush, too much guff, too much altogether'

We have stressed the importance of being aware that your personal statement is a performance where you are being judged on the basis of your ability to sell a good impression of yourself in correct English. What we must add is that some applicants – and this applies at every level from applying to university through to applying for a place on an employer's graduate trainee scheme – in their anxiety to avoid dashing off something that looks carelessly written, rush to the opposite extreme, going over the top with a display of literary fireworks. What do we mean by this? Consider the opening words of this university application:

> The writings of literature enable me to explore the labyrinth that is the human mind in intimate detail. As a child I craved the diversion and thrill of narrative. Then a love of classic books at an early age triggered my interest in literature and allowed me to develop a strong, sharp imagination. My enquiring mind and inquisitive nature therefore draw me to English Literature as a subject. Day by day I discover afresh how the English language is both beautiful and complex.

We asked an admissions tutor in the university where we teach to express his view about this kind of application. He summed it up in a few words: 'Too much gush, too much guff, too much altogether.' The applicant goes on and on, waxing lyrical but also, seemingly, trying to batter us into submission. He is a very good applicant (who would have been offered a place), but his statement hinders rather than helps his cause.

But what exactly is going wrong? Let's start with judging the conventions of the exercise. In a sense the student has got it right here, in that he is selling himself, but there is also a question of tone. The question of tone is a central consideration when we revise and edit our work. This statement is in some respects extremely well written, in that the spelling, punctuation and syntax are accurate. But part of the activity of editing involves ensuring that expression brings the ideas into focus, rather than the expression itself being the main thing that strikes the reader. This involves such things as cutting back on excessive use of adjectives, and simply losing words in sentences that go on for too long. Look at how many words can be lost in 'The writings of literature enable me to explore the labyrinth that is the human mind in intimate detail.' It is a sentence that is straining in its desire to impress, but it is a sentence that would actually make far more of an impact if it was more direct. It could be stripped back to: 'Literature enables me to explore the human mind.' Form must serve content; in the original version of this sentence, rhetoric obscures meaning. The applicant is trying to sound sophisticated, but it is the simpler version of the sentence that actually sounds like the work of a mature mind.

▶ 16 How to impress: be organised, direct and clear

How does one go about putting a statement together? First, grasp the nature of the exercise, which is to sell yourself. Do some initial planning; you might decide on a subject focus for each paragraph. Then, write a clear account of yourself, preferably in three economical paragraphs. Don't go on for too long; accept that your statement will probably work better if you cut out some of the things you might have included. Finally, make sure that your use of English is accurate; this will involve reading and re-reading sentences out loud to yourself until they sound and look right. You might also want to tinker with and rearrange the order of sentences. If you are studying for your A-levels, remember that your university application is one of the most important things you will ever write. You must take time over it. You may be able to submit your application electronically, something that can lead to increased sloppiness in framing personal statements. Don't write your statement directly onto the website without drafting it first (the same point applies to all applications); your statement is something you need to have laboured over and really worked on before submitting the application.

Here is an applicant who manages to sell herself to prospective universities in a very effective way. In this statement, the admissions tutor can take everything in quickly and easily. At the same time, the positive way in which the student has met the challenge of framing the statement will lead the admissions tutor to feel confident that the applicant will display equally admirable qualities when she embarks upon a university degree.

Why French? The main reason for choosing French is that I enjoy the subject immensely. I have studied French at GCSE and A-level and have always appreciated the lively debates and opportunity for independent study that the subject offers. My A-level studies have helped me to develop an open approach to French literature. For example, I was surprised by the humour of the Molière texts. My interest in literature is not focused on one period, author or form as I like variety in my reading. I have also developed an interest in researching the historical background of the authors and their works. The added depth that this can bring to the study of French literature is very satisfying.

<u>Why You?</u> All the individual French courses I have chosen stood out because of the variety and scope they allow for individual choice. The flexibility they offer in shaping a degree is very appealing. Added to this, all the universities I have chosen offer other Modern Language opportunities and have good Information Technology facilities. At the moment, I do not have a specific career course in mind, but I feel that a degree course in French offers the opportunity to acquire skills that are highly valued by employers.

<u>Why Me?</u> As well as studying for my degree course, I am also looking forward to participating in university life. I realise the value of taking part in extra activities and have been involved in many aspects of my school community. For example, I have helped organise and run senior citizen parties, and I have taken a central role in a school production of *A Midsummer Night's Dream*. I have also acted as an 'ambassador' for the school, showing round prospective pupils. In my free time I enjoy playing the flute and am currently working towards my Grade Eight.

We are not suggesting that everyone should adopt the format of this particular application, but it must be clear that the student has grasped the nature of the exercise and its implicit expectations. She makes her case as effectively as an advertisement might make its sales pitch. There is a strong paragraph logic in evidence here: each of the three paragraphs has a purpose, and sticks to that purpose. And then, in the body of each of the three paragraphs, enough is said to create interest without the paragraphs in any sense outstaying their welcome. One final point: you might like to note that of all the applications looked at so far in this chapter, this is in a number of respects the simplest. Sentence structure is clear and uncluttered. The paragraphs develop the case in a clear and direct way. But, as simple as it is, it is the most impressive of the personal statements. This is something to bear in mind in everything you write. Try to avoid becoming ensnarled in complicated sentences and convoluted lines of thought. Everything you want to say can be expressed in clear and simple sentences.

▶ **17 Interpreting advice**

It is often the case, when applying to a university, for a job, and in other situations, that advice will be provided about how to complete the form. Obviously, you need to pay attention to this advice. But sometimes words of guidance do need to be treated with a degree of caution.

University UCAS forms, for example, come with a booklet that offers some advice about how to make your personal statement. The problem is that the advice given does not tally entirely with the task of actually writing the statement. The UCAS form suggests that when you write your statement you include some or all of the following points:

1. Why you have chosen the courses you have listed.
2. Why you are interested in the subject.
3. Any job, work experience, placement or voluntary work you have done, particularly if it is relevant to your subject.
4. Details of key skills you have gained through, for example, General National Vocational Qualifications (GNVQ), etc.
5. Other achievements, such as the Duke of Edinburgh's Award etc.
6. Particular interests you have in your current studies.
7. Your future plans.
8. Any subjects you are studying that do not have an exam.
9. Any sponsorship or placements you have or have applied for.
10. If you are planning to take a year out, your reasons why.
11. Your social, sports or leisure interests.

One aspect of this list is very helpful. You are encouraged to focus on tangible things. The admissions tutor does not want to read vague waffle about your love of the subject. You need to include hard facts and information in your statement. This is the case in all forms of writing. Don't flap about with vague gestures; make everything as concrete as possible. Don't just say you enjoy reading; say what books you have enjoyed reading. Don't just say you play an active part in the life of your local church; provide a specific example. As far as possible, your writing in any context should always be fact-based in this kind of way.

What is less helpful about UCAS's university application advice, however, is that it might encourage a long and shapeless statement, or possibly even a statement of eleven paragraphs in which the applicant feels obliged to make some reference to every single point. What you need to recognise is that the official advice suggests what you might put into the paragraphs of your statement but does not provide any kind of suggestion about how you might construct a neat and effective application plan. What we have suggested is that you think in terms of a three-paragraph structure. That creates an immediate impression of coherence and organisation. The logic continues in the idea that you introduce yourself in the first paragraph (more or less, 'Hello, this is me, and I want to come to your university to study your subject'), you go into more detail in the next paragraph ('You might be wondering why you should select me. Well, I have a lot of good qualities'), and then in the final paragraph you say that there might be some more things the university needs to know before offering you a place ('I'm not just an academic whiz but an all-round wonderful and interesting person as well').

How long should each paragraph go on for? Well, just as three paragraphs overall provides a neat 'beginning, middle and end' structure, it makes sense to think of each paragraph dividing into three steps. Lots of people write lots and lots of sentences; after a while, the sentences don't make any impact because they are simply accumulating to very little purpose. But if you think in terms of three steps in each paragraph (some of which might be more than one sentence), and each of these steps serving a purpose, then your statement should make a real impact. As soon as you begin to think in this manner, you aren't just filling space but crafting something. In a crafted piece of writing, every paragraph, every sentence and every word contributes meaningfully to the statement as a whole.

▶ 18 The master plan: three paragraphs, and three steps in each paragraph

Here is another personal statement from a university application form. This is a very good candidate, who was offered a place. Her statement supports her case, and contributed to her being offered a place, but there is at the same time a sense of opportunities being wasted here. A small amount of reorganisation and structuring could turn this into a statement that really arrests the attention of the admissions tutor. The main problem with this as a piece of writing is that it straggles through too many short paragraphs. Inevitably, the impression is of a statement that is bitty and shapeless; by the end, it looks like a list:

My choice to pursue English at degree level has developed from the enjoyment and success that I have gained from my study of languages throughout my school career. English past and present is my particular interest and this has been nurtured by the texts that I have studied which fascinate me, such as *The Woman in White* and the poems of Philip Larkin. I have extended my reading to explore a range of novels which include *Tess of the D'Urbervilles* and *The Bell Jar*. I participate enthusiastically in discussing and learning more about these topics.

I realise that I still have much to learn and that I would like to further deepen and expand my knowledge by taking my passion for English to a higher level.

Within school I have taken part in an intensive Shakespeare course which has led me to relish the chance of studying his works. Through my love of books and reading, I have become a school librarian.

To balance my academic studies, I volunteered as a House Charity Representative in order to raise money for the children in an African village, this involved running a number of fund-raising events.

I have enjoyed being the main organiser of a school Fashion Show, raising money for charitable causes.

For the past few years, I have been a member of the school swimming squad.

Outside of school, I am a keen swimmer and tennis player. I hope to compete for my county at one of these sports and continue with it at university.

My love of outdoor pursuits has been recognised by my achieving both the Bronze and silver Duke of Edinburgh Award, and I am now working towards the Gold.

I feel that my experiences both inside school and outside school, have aided my development as a well-rounded and interesting person with much to offer when starting university.

The problem is solved as soon as we begin to apply the 'rule of three': organising the statement into three paragraphs, and, as far as is practically or reasonably possible, trying to get three main points in each paragraph. At the same time we have lost words; for example, the wordiness of the opening phrase, 'My choice to pursue English'. This is typical of the manner in which students try to sound more mature by using too many words, whereas it is the plain statement that actually sounds more mature:

> My choice of English at degree level is based upon the enjoyment and success that I have gained from my study of the subject at school. My interest has been nurtured by the texts I have studied, particularly *The Woman in White* and the poems of Philip Larkin. I also thoroughly enjoyed an intensive Shakespeare course. Beyond the A-level syllabus, I have read a range of novels including *Tess of the D'Urbervilles* and *The Bell Jar*. I realise, however, that I still have much to learn, and would like to extend my knowledge by pursuing my interest in English at a higher level.
>
> My love of books and reading has led to me becoming a school librarian. To complement my academic studies, I volunteered as a House Charity Representative in order to raise money for the children in an African village. This involved running a number of fund-raising events. In a similar area, I have enjoyed being the main organiser of a school Fashion Show which raised money for charitable causes. For some years, I have been a member of the school swimming squad.
>
> Outside of school, I am a keen swimmer and tennis player. I hope to compete for my county at one of these sports and continue with it at university. I have gained both the Bronze and Silver Duke of Edinburgh Awards, and I am now working towards the Gold. I feel that I am a well-rounded and interesting person, with much to offer when starting university.

We won't bother to point out all the little changes we have made, as what we really want to draw attention to is the overall logic. The student introduces herself, fills out the story and then finishes off with some additional information that tells us more about her as a rounded personality. Try to see as well how, in tightening up the sentence structure, we have tried to ensure that every sentence adds something really tangible to the overall story. The reference now says less but at the same time says more.

We might add that a great many of the references that schools and colleges provide on university application forms would make more of an impact if they were also organised into three purposeful sections, beginning with the applicant's school record to date, followed by their performance in the sixth form and likely performance in A-levels, and their personality and interests. It is all too often the case that admissions tutors have to plough through extremely long and poorly organised references. Schools are naturally keen to support their students, but sometimes referees could help an applicant's cause more by saying less. A reference that spills over the edge of the form or is so crowded that it becomes unreadable is self-defeating.

▶ 19 Cutting/editing

There are two ways of writing anything. It is possible to build carefully, making sure that every word that you add to the overall structure is exactly the right word in exactly the right place. Most people do things round the other way, however, writing a great deal, and then trying to organise and discipline what they have written. This is the situation you might well find yourself in. You might have written down everything you can think to say about yourself, and so have a huge statement that has to be cut down to size. It is also possible, however, that you might be at a loss as to what to say. Whereas some people applying to university have travelled the world, doing loads of good work for charity and representing their school at every conceivable sport, you might have done very little apart from your homework. If this is the case, you have to make your academic work the focus of what you write about. But not in a vague way; there is no point in waffling about how much the subject means to you and how you relish the prospect of pursuing it further. You need to write in a precise way, with lots of facts, names of books you have read and references to things and ideas you are interested in.

Even if you follow this advice, however, there is a chance that you might end up with a statement a little like the one below, a statement that contains a lot of waffle and bluster, and which cries out to be cut and made sharper. This is the first paragraph of the original, where the applicant deals with his enjoyment of English. He then had a paragraph about his other activities in school, and a paragraph about his other interests. The overall pattern of the statement was, therefore, extremely well organised. But the applicant should have cut back on the unnecessary words in each sentence. Time and time again, students add an adjective, thinking that a descriptive word enhances the weightiness of what they are saying, whereas the usual effect is to weaken the overall impression:

> My long-standing and heart-felt desire to study the subject of English at university is derived from my deep love of literature. I avidly read both poetry

and prose as a source of enjoyment and regard literature as thought provoking in its development of the imagination. I look forward to studying English at university as I find the expression of human thought, emotion and experience fascinating. I have enjoyed reading for pleasure since a young age and studying English at A-level has encouraged me to broaden the amount of books I have read, and to appreciate a higher quality of text. I enjoy current modern contemporary literature, particularly by female authors such as Doris Lessing, Jeanette Winterson and both poetry and prose by Sylvia Plath, and I have enjoyed Vikram Seth and Salman Rushdie. I have an interest in Shakespeare, which has led me to see two productions this year.

The applicant needs to cut the waffle. Some parts of this paragraph can disappear entirely. But there are also plenty of facts and names here; these need to be retained and given greater prominence.

My desire to study English at university is based upon my love of literature. I enjoy reading both poetry and prose, and look forward to studying English at university as there are so many books that I want to read. Studying English at A-level has started to introduce me to the huge range of works. Apart from the A-level set texts, I enjoy contemporary literature, particularly by female authors such as Doris Lessing and Jeanette Winterson; I have also read both the poetry and prose of Sylvia Plath. Other writers I have found interesting are Vikram Seth and Salman Rushdie. I also enjoy drama, and have seen two Shakespeare productions this year.

This represents a substantial rewriting of the applicant's opening paragraph, yet in a way the changes are minor. The intention, and effect, is to present a sharper sense of the applicant. The way in which the improved version has been brought about is by tinkering with the original draft, thinking about the logic, sequence, length and tone of the sentences. In a sense, all that is involved is the recognition that there is always an additional stage in writing. This is reading over and reflecting on what you have written, seeing if you can find a way of saying more by saying less.

▶ 20 Applying for a job

This section of the book is about how to apply for a job as well as being about how to apply for a course, but we aren't going to add too much specifically on applying for a job because everything we have said so far applies equally here. You need to sell yourself – neatly and convincingly. The form of what you write is just as important as the content. Accuracy and correctness are vital. Often, potential employers ask you to submit a letter (sometimes a hand-written letter) along with your CV. You can see what they are interested in. Has this applicant taken the trouble to write carefully (or have they dashed something off as quickly as possible)? You don't need to write at length. As with a university application, an application that consists of three paragraphs with approximately three points in each paragraph is likely to make the strongest impression. Paragraph 1 introduces your reason for writing, paragraph 2 adds relevant information that will strengthen your case, and paragraph 3 adds anything extra that might be relevant.

In paragraph 3 you will also want to take your leave. This can often prove a little tricky in terms of getting the tone right. You shouldn't really write: 'A swift response to this letter would be appreciated.' That is the wrong tone – and tone is always important in writing. Rather than ending with you making demands upon the recipient of your letter, it is much better to end with the suggestion that you are always happy to be of service. You might conclude by saying: 'If there is any further information you require, I will, of course, be happy to forward it immediately.'

In order to demonstrate the way in which the rule of three operates when applying for a job, we would like you to consider this letter of application. The person who wrote this had graduated from university a year before writing the letter, and, consequently, at this time had less than a year's track record in employment, but the letter creates an impression of an applicant with tremendous experience and expertise.

Please find enclosed my application for the position of Assistant Administrator in the Department of Employment and Services. I have recent experience of working as an administrator in a medium-sized office dealing with management issues and also official documents from local government. The post has given me an insight into the workings of the public sector and its legal responsibilities as well as its complex workload.

The skills that I would bring to the new post include excellent communication skills, ranging from representing my employer at public meetings, training new staff and developing newsletters to writing information sheets for staff. I have good IT skills and can use a range of packages, including word processing and data bases. I am proficient in the use of the internet and my present post makes me responsible for co-ordinating the department intranet for strategic purposes.

I have a sound basic knowledge of industrial relations and a commitment to public service ideals. I am familiar with issues such as the need for strategic planning, managing change and policy development. I have good personal organisational skills and place an importance on clear, tactful communication skills in the sections I currently administer. If there is any further information you require, I will, of course, be happy to forward it immediately.

It would be possible to turn all the points listed here into bullet points, but in most applications for most jobs what is required is a letter that demonstrates that the writer can actually write. Your CV will show that you can organise material under headings and place facts in the appropriate place, but where a letter is required you need to sell yourself clearly and accurately. As with the application to university, try to be as factual as possible. There is no point in exaggerating your achievements or skills since an interviewer will soon find you out. Weigh what you say carefully and present it clearly so that you can speak about it later – when you are interviewed. You will be surprised how much you can say in a short space and how persuasive this will be when weighed against other, more waffly, applications.

Questions of tone – of how you address people and what kind of language you use and the impact it has – are something that we will return to. In the next section, however, we want to deal with the most fundamental issue of all: what you write will have no real value unless it is written in grammatically correct English.

3 Writing Correct and Convincing Sentences

▶ 21 The sentence secret: keep it simple

The core unit in writing is the sentence. It is impossible to produce effective work if one cannot produce mechanically correct sentences. When writing goes wrong – for example, when someone fails to say what they were trying to say – it is usually because the construction of the individual sentence has gone wrong. Generating effective sentences should, of course, be the easiest task in the world; after all, we all manage to do it thousands of times a day when we are speaking. But when it comes to putting words on paper, generating effective sentences is an activity that everyone finds a challenge.

Why should this be so? One reason may be because we normally talk in a rather lazy way, using gesture, emphasis and tone of voice to clarify the sense of what we are saying. The written sentence, by contrast, has to be disciplined, structured and self-sufficient. The difference between spoken and written language is in some ways like the difference between fast food and a sensible diet: writing demands a little more thought and a little more restraint. But it is well worth accepting the challenge of trying to improve the quality of your sentences. What makes the challenge less daunting is the fact that when people make mistakes they always make the same mistakes, or, to simplify just a little, we could say that they make just one mistake: they don't write sentences that are short, simple and direct. As we pointed out in Section 1, it is the weakest candidates sitting secondary school exams such as GCSE English who write the longest sentences. The better candidates have grasped the idea of controlling and limiting sentence length; they have probably realised that a short sentence makes a far more forceful impression on the reader than a long sentence.

Consider the openings of these classic novels. George Eliot's *Middlemarch* begins: 'Miss Brooke had that kind of beauty which seems to be thrown into relief by poor dress.' Thomas Hardy's *Tess of the d'Urbervilles* starts: 'On an evening in the latter part of May a middle-aged man was walking homeward from Shaston to the village of Marlott, in the adjoining Vale of Blakemore or Blackmoor.' Neither author offers anything in the way of a fancy flourish. Instead, they concentrate on presenting the reader with information in a clear and direct manner (although the fact is that both sentences, in a subtle way, start to establish the central themes of their respective novels). When you are writing, it is a good idea to start with a sentence that very simply, and not outstaying its welcome, makes a bold opening statement. Don't go on for too long. Look at this, the opening of Benjamin Disraeli's novel *Coningsby*:

> It was a bright May morning some twelve years ago, when a youth of still tender age, for he had certainly not entered his teens by more than two years, was ushered into the waiting-room of a house in the vicinity of St. James's Square, which, though with the general appearance of a private residence, and that too of no very ambitious character, exhibited at this period symptoms of being occupied for some public purpose.

In some ways this is very effective; it does present a lot of information. But it feels long-winded. A shorter opening sentence would have made more impact.

The opening sentences of classic novels might seem quite remote from the task of writing essays, but the fact is that a great many students go wrong at the outset by straining to say too much in the first sentence. Look at this example:

> Although the early Victorian period was one of change and growth, Victorian society as a whole at this time conveyed an impression of order and respectability, with life still held together through Christian moral teaching, with an emphasis placed on the virtues of monogamy and family life.

This, like the opening of Disraeli's novel, says too much in one sentence; the student is trying too hard to appear knowledgeable. But if she simplified things, making cuts and switching to two sentences, what she is saying would carry more authority. The directness of the phrasing could arrest the reader's attention:

> Although the early Victorian period was one of change and growth, society at this time conveyed an impression of order. Life was still held together by Christian teaching, with an emphasis on the virtues of marriage and family life.

The changes might seem almost inconsequential, but in the revised version there is an emphasis on delivering the material clearly to the reader.

What lessons can be drawn from this? Write in short sentences! And if you are at all unhappy with what you have written in an essay, try shortening and simplifying the sentences, particularly at the start of the essay. The paradoxical outcome should be that simpler sentences actually make your work sound more complex. Once you have tidied up your opening sentences, you will probably want to continue doing so with the sentences throughout your essay.

How to make a good start when writing

1. Write short, clear and direct sentences.

2. Be prepared to cut and edit what you have written in order to produce short, clear and direct sentences.

▶ 22 Sentences: the terms you need to know

Brevity is the first principle of sentence construction. But your ability to write effectively will also be enhanced if you know a little about the mechanics of a sentence. This is the point at which some readers will decide to skip a few pages in this book. They have realised over the years that everything written about grammar is deadly dull. We aren't, however, going to drone on at great length. All we want to do is to present the facts about the structure of sentences that can prove directly helpful in strengthening your writing.

At primary school, pupils are sometimes told that a sentence is 'a collection of about ten words that makes sense'. This might not be the technical definition, and a lot of sentences will be much longer, but it points us in the right direction: a sentence is a complete thought expressed in words. It begins with a capital letter and ends with a full stop. What we can also say about a sentence is that it:

• gives expression to a subject which the writer wishes to draw the reader's attention to; and
• tells the reader about that subject.

It follows from this that a sentence has two parts to it. If we write '*has some computer games', for example, it is not a complete sentence (although it might be comprehensible in conversation). Something is missing. What is missing is the **subject**. If we write 'The girl has some computer games', we have formed a complete sentence: our attention is drawn to the girl (the subject of the sentence), and then something is said about her. This second part of the sentence is called the **predicate**. This is the first point to grasp, that we can describe the basic structure of a sentence as having two parts: a subject and a predicate.

Here are some very straightforward examples of the subject/predicate pattern: 'His laughter / was hysterical', 'We / drank the pub dry', 'Who / told you?' The majority of written sentences, in fact, never become much more complicated than these examples. The logic of sentence structure – and of effective writing – is particularly clear in proverbs. These are short, pithy sayings in general use. It is nearly always the case that they conform to the pattern of a clear-cut subject and then a predicate that completes the sentence in a neat fashion. But what the person interested in good writing is also likely to notice is just how economically they use words in order to make a point in a manner that commands the reader's attention:

Too many cooks / spoil the broth.

A stitch in time / saves nine.

He who hesitates / is lost.

A bird in the hand / is worth two in the bush.

You might notice that in these proverbs the subject of the sentence is not a single word such as 'We' but a group of words that form a single unit or topic: 'Too many cooks'; 'He who hesitates'. The subject is the topic we are writing about.

This might seem a lot to take in, but all we have said is that a sentence tells us something about a subject. But you might be wondering about **verbs**. Where do they fit into this pattern of subject and predicate? Don't sentences need verbs? Yes, they do. The verb is part of the predicate. If we go back to our example, this should become clear if we omit the verb:

*The girl / some computer games.

We still have a subject – 'The girl' – and we still have a predicate – 'some computer games'. But the sentence no longer makes sense; it is not a proper sentence because it lacks the verb, 'has'. The verb is a key part of the predicate since it tells us the key information about what is going on. If we changed the verb to 'stole' we would alter the whole meaning of the sentence, but not its structure.

Grammar, a topic that seems to inspire an inordinate amount of dread in many people, is simply a way of describing how the parts of a sentence fit together. The two basic parts, as we have seen, are the subject and predicate. The predicate itself can be divided into two basic parts, the verb and the rest of the words:

> Too many cooks / spoil the broth.

Here the verb is 'spoil' while 'the broth' is the **object**. You can identify the object by asking who or what was affected by the verb. Many sentences follow exactly this pattern: they have a subject and a predicate, and the predicate is made up of a verb and an object. The only real exceptions are sentences such as 'He who hesitates is lost', where the verb 'is' cannot have an object. Instead, we call 'lost' a **complement**. A number of verbs are like the verb 'to be' (here in the form of 'is'), where nothing is affected by them: 'that *sound*s good'; 'I *felt* tired'; 'you *seem* happy'; 'he *became* angry'. In all these cases we talk about complements ('good', 'tired', 'happy', 'angry') rather than objects. The term 'complement' means 'something that completes the sentence'.

For the most part in the discussion below we are going to refer simply to subject and predicate (or sometimes subject, verb and object) because these are the core elements of the sentence. We will refer to other grammatical terms, but our real concern is with the basic workings of the sentence and how to manage and control your writing. Knowing some terms can help in this if it helps you identify how to improve what you have to say, but getting a feel for the workings of language is just as important.

▶ 23 Enlarging a sentence

When sentences go wrong, it is usually because the kind of simplicity of structure (subject plus predicate) outlined above becomes obscured. Theoretically, therefore, we could all become better writers if we simply wrote in short sentences all the time. And there is a lot to be said for writing in short sentences as much as one can. But if every sentence was short, writing would start to resemble that limited command of other languages most of us display on foreign holidays, where we attempt little more than basic statements. We might be able to order a beer in another country, but we would find it hard going to discuss the finer points of that country's culture. In order to say everything we want to say in a piece of writing, our sentences have to expand. The secret involved here is knowing how to handle this expansion. As you start to add extra bits to your sentences, it helps if you are aware that you are working in accordance with a generally recognised set of rules.

The smallest additions to sentences are **descriptive words**. In the **simple** sentence 'The cat sat on the mat,' the cat is the subject ('simple' here means a sentence made up of one independent **main clause** only: one group of words containing a subject and a predicate). The word 'cat' is also a **noun**, which is a word that names a person, place or thing. If we decide to expand the sentence, by saying 'The lazy cat sat on a Persian mat,' the words 'lazy' and 'Persian' are **adjectives**. That is to say, they are words whose function is to modify – describe or define more precisely – the nouns used.

We might also enlarge a sentence by using other nouns to explain the existing nouns in a sentence: 'Stephen Knight, the detective, arrested the murderer, Norman Thomas.' These nouns – 'the detective', 'Norman Thomas' – are said to be in **apposition**. We refer to them as **appositives**: they are words or phrases that follow a noun to define, identify or rename it. In this example, 'Stephen Knight' is pinned down as 'the detective', but then, in the second half of the sentence, 'the murderer' is pinned down as 'Norman Thomas'. Adjectives and appositives are added to nouns.

Adverbs are words that qualify the meaning of any word in a sentence apart from a noun (or **pronoun**, such as 'he' or 'they'), although they can modify the meaning of a whole clause or sentence. Adverbs are the easiest words to identify in a sentence as they nearly always ending in 'ly', as in 'The cat sat lazily on the mat.' When we referred to the 'lazy cat', it was an adjective, as it described the noun 'cat', but now 'lazily' describes how the cat was sitting; it modifies the verb 'sat'. An adverb can, however, modify a whole sentence. For example, a wrestler might declare: 'Finally, the Rock has come back to New York City.' The adverb here is 'Finally'.

Sentences can also be enlarged by small clusters of words that add to or modify the sense of the sentence as a whole. These clusters are either **phrases** or **clauses**. A phrase is a group of words that forms a unit of meaning but does not contain a verb. It is often the case that phrases locate or position the material in the sentence. For example,

'*In the afternoon*, John usually has a short sleep,' '*By the station*, a blind musician played a mournful tune.'

A clause is a more substantial addition to a sentence; as with a phrase, it is usually signposted by the presence of commas. If you were reading a sentence out loud, an introductory clause would end where you took a very short pause before moving to the body of the sentence (as in this current sentence). But the supplementary clause could also appear at the end of the sentence, after a comma, or in the middle of a sentence, between commas. A clause, as it usually includes a subject and a predicate, can sometimes stand as a sentence in its own right, but more often than not it only makes sense in the context of the main proposition in a sentence. Here is an example: 'Jill's hospital appointment, *which was scheduled for late April*, was delayed by six months.' The clause is the bit between commas in the middle of the sentence.

That last example provides a good instance of the way in which we can make use of a handful of moves to add elegance and variety to what we are writing. We could write three sentences: 'Jill had a hospital appointment. It was scheduled for late April. It was delayed by six months.' At a slightly more ambitious level – the level at which young children tell stories – we could combine two or more sentences by using words such as 'and', 'but', 'or', 'nor', 'for', 'yet' and 'so'. These seven words are the main ways of joining sentences together and are called **co-ordinating conjunctions**: 'Jill had a hospital appointment, and it was scheduled for late April, but it was delayed by six months.' This is a **compound sentence**, a sentence that combines two, or more than two, simple sentences. A sentence that joins two sentences together can also be called a **double sentence**: 'Jill had a hospital appointment, and it was scheduled for late April.' Notice that when we join two sentences together what we end up with is two **main clauses**, two groups of words that could stand on their own as sentences.

What we originally wrote, however, is referred to as a **complex sentence**: 'Jill's hospital appointment, which was scheduled for late April, was delayed by six months.' It is complex because it absorbs an additional clause (or clauses) into its structure; we use the term **subordinate clause** for the additional clause in the body of the sentence. It is subordinate because it depends on the main clause and can't stand on its own as a sentence: '*which was scheduled for late April' doesn't make any sense by itself. As we noted at the end of the last section, though, knowing terms is less important than recognising what's going on in a sentence. All the time, what you are looking at is ways of combining words into larger units. But we always start with the basics: 'The cat sat on the mat.' This is a perfectly good sentence with a clear subject/predicate structure that can be added to in straightforward ways.

▶ 24 If it is so easy, why is it so hard?

It might surprise you to discover that the previous unit provided an exhaustive list of the ways in which we can complicate an English sentence. What writing involves is writing a simple opening sentence, and then moving on to slightly more complicated sentences (but never hesitating to use a short sentence when a short sentence works best). Sentences should never be unduly or awkwardly long. If extra information is required in the middle of a sentence, we should usually be able to signal its introduction with a comma, and then, with another comma, signal our return to the main thrust of the sentence. It really is as simple as that. Why, therefore, do so many people find writing so difficult?

There is a chicken-and-egg dilemma involved here. A lot of students are struggling to write at the limits of what they can manage at that stage of their education; they are rather like athletes running as fast as possible. Because they are having difficulty formulating ideas in their minds, their confusion spills over into what they are writing on the page. Everything is just a little bit strained, and at this point the logic of sentence writing disintegrates. But what you need to realise is that just a little more awareness of the rules of sentence construction can help you express the most complex ideas with ease. In chaotic writing, the subject and predicate of the main part of the sentence are likely to become bewilderingly separated from each other, and additional clauses are likely to creep in at the wrong point or without proper signposts, which means commas, to mark their arrival. You also need to tell yourself that one sentence can only say so much. If you have got a long and involved sentence, there is every possibility that splitting the sentence into two (or even three) separate sentences, in which the subject/predicate sequence is a little plainer, will clarify what you are attempting to say. Similarly, if you lose some words from a sentence, making its subject/predicate pattern plainer, and being in control of any deviation into a subordinate clause, this will sort out both your ideas and the quality of the expression of your ideas.

What are the practical implications of this advice? When you have written something, look again and see whether you can proceed through the tangled path you might have established in a more measured way. Time and time again, it is just such steady restraint that students lack in their writing. It is always the case that the students who will do best are the students who are brave enough to put their trust in simple and clear sentences. They have sensed that they can impress with the steady development of an argument, rather than throwing too much into each and every sentence.

▶ 25 Clustering, enlarging, cutting

If you have written something and feel happy with what you have written, you can forget about any possible problems and move on. This might be the case if, for example, you are writing a letter to a friend; the message that you want to send is straightforward, and you have not encountered any difficulty in conveying it. Problems in writing start when you are trying to express an idea that taxes your brain. It as at this point that sentences begin to crumble; they become awkward as they fail to say what you want them to say. And even if you get the whole essay written, you might feel that a lot of the sentences need to be returned to and polished.

It is at such points – when you are having difficulty framing a sentence or when you want to check a sentence you have written – that it helps if you call upon three check words: **clustering**, **enlarging** and **cutting**. First, you have to check the core structure of the sentence, looking at where and how the main idea clusters. Then you need to do a spot check on complications, asides and additions you have built into the sentence: have these been kept under control, with proper signals (i.e. commas) to the reader when signals are deemed necessary? Finally, you must check – by losing words if possible – that every word you have used actually contributes to the clear meaning of the sentence; it is often the case that an excess of words in a sentence can obscure its meaning, and that some of the words will be serving no real function.

First, **clustering**. A sentence always works best if you and your reader can spot the core element – the subject and predicate – and if these elements of the sentence are kept fairly close to each other. Consider the following: 'Queen Victoria / reigned for over sixty years.' Here we have the usual sequence of subject/predicate. The sequence of the sentence can also be referred to as subject/verb/complement, as seen here: 'Queen Victoria [**subject**] reigned [**verb**] for over sixty years [**complement**].' A sentence will usually be at its clearest if the subject is immediately followed by the verb, and if the subject and verb are expressed as simply as possible. Long intrusions between subject and verb can obscure meaning. 'Queen Victoria, in an era that witnessed extraordinary levels of change, especially a massive movement from agriculture to industry at the heart of the British economy, as many have pointed out in accounts of her life, reigned for over sixty years.' The naïve writer might be tempted to opt for a long sentence, feeling that it sounds more ambitious. But it doesn't work, as the reader loses sight of the subject of the sentence.

The example we have used could be even more complicated: 'Any study of the nineteenth century must start with the fact that Queen Victoria, in an era that witnessed extraordinary levels of change, especially a massive movement from agriculture to industry at the heart of the British economy, as many have pointed out in accounts of her life, reigned for over sixty years.' But try to keep to simple sentences if you can: 'Queen Victoria reigned for over sixty years.' If you are interested in enlarging this sentence, where is the additional information going to appear? Most of the time you would make such additions unconsciously, but sometimes you have to think about how and where you are **enlarging** the sentence.

It could be at the start, as a positioning or placing gesture: 'In an era that witnessed extraordinary levels of change, Queen Victoria reigned for over sixty years.' Can you see how this supports rather than obscures the main element of the sentences? But you might choose to add words after the main clause: 'Queen Victoria reigned for over sixty years, establishing a sense of stability and continuity in an era of change.' Or a subordinate phrase could be hammocked in the sentence. 'Queen Victoria, short, plump and seldom amused, reigned for over sixty years.' You might want to note here that when there are words between the subject and the verb they are often in apposition, that is to say renaming, in the sense of telling us more about, the subject of the sentence (here, that Victoria was short, plump and seldom amused).

What you need to recognise is that the rules about enlarging a sentence are very straightforward: you can insert extra words at the beginning, in the middle or at the end of a sentence. More often than not the addition or enlargement is signalled to the reader by a comma or commas. If you are having difficulty enlarging a sentence, push the material into a second sentence: 'Any study of the nineteenth century must start with the fact that Queen Victoria reigned for over sixty years. It was an era that witnessed extraordinary levels of change, especially a massive movement from agriculture to industry at the heart of the British economy.' But then you need to ask yourself if the sentences are saying what they have to say as fluently and effectively as possible.

It is at this stage that **cutting** might be a good idea: 'Queen Victoria reigned for over sixty years. This era witnessed extraordinary levels of change, especially a massive movement from agriculture to industry at the heart of the British economy.' The reduced version might have lost some of the shades of meaning of the first version, but it gains rather more in terms of clarity and directness. The three moves we have described here are very simple but they are the three steps necessary in converting sentences that don't work into sentences that do work. If you have written an essay and want to redraft and polish it, you need to go through the essay making sure that you have got the core of each sentence clearly identified (clustering), that you are in charge of additions to and complications within sentences (enlarging), and that you have got rid of superfluous words (cutting). There is another step in writing, which is mastering the art of developing and sustaining an argument, but that is something we turn to later in the book when we start to discuss the theory and practice of essay structure.

▶ 26 Make sure that your sentences really are sentences: the problem of fragments

Sentences can go wrong because they become convoluted, but there are two other errors that often appear in students' essays: the fragment and the comma splice. We want to focus on the fragment in this unit. A sentence consists of a subject and predicate. Every sentence must contain at least one main clause, with its own **finite verb**. (For example, in 'I love flowers' the finite verb is 'love'. The term 'finite' is discussed below, but it means the verb form that agrees with the subject, not the *ing* or *to* form: '*I to love flowers' is not a proper sentence.) Additional and subordinate clauses may be added, but are not compulsory. It is subjects and verbs that are the basic building blocks of sentences. But quite often when students are writing, this happens:

> Steve Smith, the legendary goal wizard, never trained for a match. *Just turned up on a Saturday and scored.

The civil war continued for nearly five years. *Until the intervention of other countries in the region.

The attendance at the Reverend Parker's first service in the new church was over two hundred. *The largest number this year.

In each case there is nothing at all wrong with the first sentence, but in each case the second 'sentence' is not actually a sentence but a fragment. These second sentences continue and seem to complete the meaning of the first sentences, but they lack a subject or lack a verb.

Sometimes this is permissible for rhetorical effect. The Reverend Parker might write in his Parish Magazine: 'The attendance at church last Sunday was over two hundred. *The largest number this year. It was extremely gratifying to see so many good souls on such a wet weekend.' This gives a very informal, almost chatty, tone, and this 'register' or form of language might seem appropriate in context. It could, though, be rewritten quite simply (and more formally) for the vicar's report to the Bishop: 'The attendance at church last Sunday was over two hundred. This represents the largest number this year. It was extremely gratifying to see so many good souls on such a wet weekend' The word 'This' in the middle sentence reintroduces a subject, while 'represents' provides the sentence with a finite verb. Fragments might strike you as a trivial thing to make a fuss about, and it is certainly the case that in casual writing, and newspapers, they appear all the time, but they are best avoided in academic or professional writing because they can interfere with your ability to express a complicated point.

▶ 27 Make sure your sentences really are sentences: the problem of the comma splice

Even more common than the use of the fragment is the use of a comma where a more substantial stop – a semicolon or a full stop – is needed. This is the separation by a comma of two clauses that are not linked by a conjunction. Examples should make the point easier to grasp:

The new approach was first introduced in selected schools in 1987, *it was in universal use by the middle of the next decade.

To make any further progress that day was impossible, *the rain was far too heavy.

Martin had collected train numbers for many years, *he claimed to have seen and photographed every train in service in England and Wales.

He had never been to Scotland, *he was unable to drive, *he had a morbid fear of travelling by rail.

He stored his photographs in leather-bound albums, *these were his most-treasured possessions.

In each of these sentences, the comma is not a heavy enough stop to 'carry' the break in the sentence. This is because the two parts are, in fact, independent main clauses; they are, that is, separate sentences, and these cannot be joined by a comma. The two clauses in each example need to be separated by a semicolon or a full stop, although there is a third possibility, which is rewriting the faulty sentence.

Look at that last sentence: 'The two clauses in each example need to be separated by a semicolon or a full stop, although there is a third possibility, which is rewriting the faulty sentence.' That is a valid and correct sentence, but what if we had written the following? 'The two clauses in each example need to be separated by a semicolon or a full stop, *there is a third possibility, which is rewriting the faulty sentence.' That would be a faulty sentence, because two separate clauses are illegitimately spliced together with a comma, whereas the version above is a legitimate sentence because it uses an additional word – 'although' – to bridge the gap.

Let's consider the bad news and the good news about comma splices. The good news about comma splices is that if you have Microsoft Word (or any other sophisticated word-processing programme) on your computer it will automatically spot comma splices if you have the 'grammatical errors' feature switched on. Be just a little cautious, however; the computer will spot what it thinks is a comma splice, but it won't always be right. The bad news about comma splices is that not everyone has Microsoft Word, nobody uses it all the time, and lots of students (and Microsoft Word) find it very hard to distinguish between a sentence with a correctly used comma and a 'sentence' that is comma-spliced.

So how do you tell the difference between correct and incorrect usage? The thing is that a comma spice relates not to a phrase or clause at the start of a sentence or to words inserted as a subordinate clause, but only to an extra bit tagged on at the end. Most commonly, if we tag an extra bit on we have to use 'and' or 'but', because we are taking things further. There are other words, such as 'although', 'whereas' and 'because' (as in the last sentence), that serve the same linking function (they are called subordinating conjunctions). We couldn't write: 'If we tag an extra bit on we often use 'and' or 'but', *we are taking things further.' Here we have just tagged on the last clause without using an extra word to signal its relationship to the material that has preceded it. We would have to write: 'If we tag an extra bit on we often use 'and' or 'but', because we are taking things further.' Or we could rewrite the sentence as two sentences: 'If we tag an extra bit on we often use 'and' or 'but'. This is because we are taking things further.' Or we could use a semicolon to separate the two sentences: 'If we tag an extra bit on we often use 'and' or 'but'; this is because we are taking things further.'

In the end it is this idea of 'tagging on' that you are probably going to have to call upon. Does it feel as if the extra bit of the sentence is just tagged on? Have I decided to extend the life and length of the sentence by first using a comma and then writing a bit more that is just tagged on? Or is it a legitimate extra bit, perhaps signalled by a word such as 'and', 'but' or 'because'? If you are in doubt, decide to divide the sentence you are unsure about into two shorter sentences. But that is not the only way of dealing with a comma splice.

▶ 28 Corrective surgery for a comma-spliced sentence (or for a 'fused' sentence)

There are four correct (and one incorrect) ways of dealing with a comma-spliced sentence, or with a 'fused' sentence, which is a variant of a comma-spliced sentence. Fused sentences are sentences where an extra clause is tagged on without even a comma signalling its arrival: '*To make any further progress that day was impossible the rain was far too heavy.' The fused sentence, even more clearly than the comma-spliced sentence, draws attention to what is going on when people make such errors. Essentially, it is a form of laziness, of just popping the words down on the page as they arrive in one's head, without thinking about the fact that a sentence has to be packaged and presented before the reader consumes it. This brings us to the first response to writing comma splices, which is that you might decide simply to ignore them.

If you want to succeed in life, however, you will want to avoid comma splices and fused sentences. You will also need to know how to correct them if they have crept into your work. There are four answers: the **full stop**, a **connecting word**, a change of **verb tense**, or a **semicolon**. Let's take an example and say that you had written the following:

> To make any further progress that day was impossible, *the rain was far too heavy.

You could rewrite this as follows:

> To make any further progress that day was impossible. The rain was far too heavy.

> To make any further progress that day was impossible, because the rain was far too heavy.

> To make any further progress that day was impossible, the rain being far too heavy.

> To make any further progress that day was impossible; the rain was far too heavy.

Don't make the mistake of thinking that a sentence with another clause stuck on at the end necessarily requires corrective surgery; if there is an 'and' or 'but' or something similar, such as 'which' or 'because', there already, the likelihood is that it does not.

When they discover that there is such a thing as the comma splice, some students become so desperate to avoid committing the error that they start over-punctuating, putting semicolons in everywhere. Remember, the semicolon is really a kind of full stop, not a kind of comma. You don't have to write the following: 'Penny was in her third year at university; *and really pleased with the flat she had that year.' That is going too far in the wrong direction, incorrectly inserting a semicolon when a comma does the job. It should be: 'Penny was in her third year at university, and really pleased with the flat she had that year.' It is a straightforward compound sentence, something that we should be able to tell by the fact that the linking word 'and' steers us from one clause to the next.

▶ 29 Taking stock: the comma splice

Can you see the logic of the corrections we have made in the following sentences (which we quoted in their incorrect forms in Unit 27)?

> (1) Martin had collected train numbers for many years. He claimed to have seen and photographed every train in service in England and Wales.

(2) He had never been to Scotland as he was unable to drive and had a morbid fear of travelling by rail.

(3) He stored his photographs in leather-bound albums; these were his most-treasured possessions.

In (1) we have used two sentences; in (2) we joined three related statements with two connecting words ('as' and 'and'), and in (3) we used a semicolon to juxtapose two related statements, both of which are main clauses. The tricky one here is the second example, where there were two commas splices. It would just be possible to write: 'He had never been to Scotland, he was unable to drive and he had a morbid fear of travelling by rail.' Here the clauses are acting as a list, with the final one joined by the 'and'. That is the only conjunction you can use to create this kind of triple sentence with the same subject – in this case, 'he'.

We will be returning to comma splices again in the course of this book, as they are probably the most common error in students' essays. But what we also want to draw attention to here is the benefit of the quick corrective surgery that gets rid of comma splices. The three sentences above in their original form sounded rather immature and careless. In their revised form, however, which has involved no more than minor tinkering with the punctuation, the sentences have acquired a degree of style in their expression. The difference between lack of success and success in writing usually depends upon making such small adjustments to individual sentences. There are rules to follow that enable you to see whether you are getting it right or not, but a great deal of this can be checked simply by reading sentences out loud to yourself, and tinkering just a little until the sentences sound as if they are doing the job competently.

▶ 30 Taking stock: keep it short, keep it simple

Remember that most additions to a simple sentence, by which we mean additional or subordinate phrases and clauses, are signalled by commas. We have touched upon the bits that come at the start of a sentence, and the bits that are added at the end, but we can also hammock bits within a sentence:

> Britain's prime ministers over the course of the latter part of the twentieth century, figures such as Margaret Thatcher, John Major and Tony Blair, who, in some respects, had a great deal in common, but, in other ways, had very few shared characteristics, were a rum lot.

The core of this long sentence is 'Britain's prime ministers over the course of the latter part of the twentieth century [subject] were [verb] a rum lot [complement].' The sentence can grow because we have signalled the additions with commas. The non-essential bits are added in a controlled way.

But we want to end with the point we have returned to again and again in this section. If a sentence becomes too elaborate, it can lose impact. It might make a lot of sense to juggle with this sentence above, in particular getting the subject and the verb closer together. That might involve shifting material into an additional sentence, with its own subject and verb.

> Britain's prime ministers over the course of the latter part of the twentieth century were a rum lot. Figures such as Margaret Thatcher, John Major and Tony Blair in some respects had a great deal in common, but in other ways they had very few shared characteristics.

What is involved in any such juggling with and rewriting of a sentence is just a little more awareness of words being like a kind of 'Lego' set. You join the pieces together, but sometimes you have to switch the pieces around if you want to build something worthwhile and which really holds together.

4 Punctuating a Sentence: Commas, Colons and Semicolons

► **31 The punctuation secret: everything else falls into place if you can use commas correctly**

If you can make yourself proficient in the handling of punctuation, you will find it possible to say exactly what you want to say. This is because punctuation is the key to precision. But, in addition, you will also start to sense that everything you write carries real conviction and authority. Above all else, what you need to get hold of is how to handle commas correctly. Commas [,] are the equivalent of changing gear when driving; you come to a point where you need to slow down a little or turn a corner. The commas help you negotiate these changes, but also, and perhaps even more importantly, they enable you to take your reader along with you. Given the importance of commas, it might seem surprising that so many people only have a vague idea how to use them, and often misuse them. We suspect that the problem is that people think there are very complicated rules about commas. But there aren't. There are just six main ways in which commas are used. Master the six rules and you will be in control of everything you write.

We turn to the first of the usages of the comma in the next unit, but first we want to provide a couple of examples of how crucial accurate punctuation is in conveying the intended meaning of a sentence. Consider this sentence, appearing first without commas: 'The England manager said David Beckham was entirely to blame for the team's dismal performance.' What do you understand the meaning of this sentence to be? It has to be that the manager of the England team criticised David Beckham. Insert two commas, however, and it is a very different story: 'The England manager, said David Beckham, was entirely to blame for the team's dismal performance.' The meaning has been reversed; it is now Beckham who is criticising the manager. The main sentence (with a slash between the subject and predicate) is 'The

England manager / was entirely to blame for the team's dismal performance.' But an additional clause – 'said David Beckham' – has been slipped into the sentence. Commas are required, however, to mark off the additional clause. If you read the sentence out loud, there is just a slight pause before and after said David Beckham. That is an important point to note. You need to know the rules about commas, but being aware of the sound pattern of a sentence helps you implement the rules.

Here is a rather more extreme example of how punctuation determines meaning. Consider this sequence of words, and then start to introduce punctuation to clarify the meaning: 'Woman without her man is nothing.' One possibility is to write 'Woman, without her man, is nothing.' In this version, the main sentence is 'Woman is nothing,' the addition suggesting that she needs her man. But we could write 'Woman! Without her, man is nothing.' The main sentence has now become 'Man is nothing,' with a recognition that he is incomplete without woman. Obviously, all unpunctuated sentences are not going to be as reversible in meaning as the examples given here, but it should be clear why punctuation matters. In particular, if you are making a fine point in an essay, it is only accurate punctuation that can negotiate nuances of meaning and make your meaning entirely clear to your readers.

▶ 32 The six uses of the comma, no. 1: punctuating linked main clauses

A lot of people tend to think that, in the past, standards in matters such as spelling, punctuation and grammar were much higher than they are today. In the course of preparing this book, however, we happened to come across a selection of writing guides published in the first half of the twentieth century. It is clear that people were experiencing exactly the same writing difficulties as they are today (and that people were also recalling a mythical golden age when everyone knew how to write correctly). One of the best things we came across in these old guides was this comment on the comma: 'The writer who handles this puny little stop correctly and sensibly can probably punctuate as well as need be.' The author went on to suggest that students who make themselves aware of how commas work then tend to get everything else right as well. What was true a hundred years ago is just as true today.

The main function of commas is that they separate information into readable units and guide the reader as to the relationship between phrases and items in a series. This starts in a very simple way as the child at primary school moves beyond simple sentences. The young child might write: 'I like pizza. Every Friday we order a takeaway. My dad orders *quattro formaggio*. He always says it is nice but rather cheesy.' If someone continued to write like this, however, it would become very tedious and jerky. What the slightly older child learns to do is to link simple sentences together into compound sentences, combining two or more linked ideas into one sentence. The sentences above could, therefore, be rewritten: 'I like pizza and every Friday we order a takeaway. My dad orders *quattro formaggio* which he always says is nice but rather cheesy.' Notice that there are no commas at the moment. Possibly they aren't really required. These are, after all, simple ideas, and there is no possibility that the reader will fail to grasp the meaning of what is being said. But including the correct punctuation removes any possibility of doubt as to the meaning of the words used. It also serves a second purpose, that of making the meaning clear to the reader at a first reading. This obviously isn't a problem here, but could be if you were writing an essay. It is, therefore, worth getting into the habit of always inserting commas where appropriate.

In this example, if we add commas the sentences become: 'I like pizza, and every Friday we order a takeaway. My dad orders *quattro formaggio*, which he always says is nice but rather cheesy.' The logic is that the separate parts of the sentence are kept separated by commas, which, at the same time, mirror the kind of momentary pause we would take in speaking the words. In other words, our speaking voice creates just enough emphasis to clarify the sense, but in the absence of a speaking voice the commas act like stage directions to the reader, explaining the sequence, order and meaning of the sentence. The first sentence above is a compound sentence (two or more simple sentences put together in a straightforward sequence), the separate parts of the sentences becoming **co-ordinate clauses**. It is often the case, as here, that such clauses are joined by 'and' or 'but'. Normally a comma is used before the 'and' or 'but', but it is superfluous when the two actions are so closely linked as to be in effect one action: 'Shop and save at Supersavers!' On other occasions you might have to decide whether a comma is required or not. It would be possible to write: 'This is the first use of the comma and it is a simple convention to grasp.' That is acceptable, because the meaning is perfectly clear, but it would be equally if not more correct (because a new subject, 'it', is introduced) to write: 'This is the first use of the comma, and it is a simple convention to grasp.' In an essay, in the course of developing an argument, there is a great deal to be said for cautiously and carefully controlling the meaning in this kind of way in every sentence.

▶ 33 The six uses of the comma, no. 2: setting off the introductory element of a sentence

This is again a case of moving beyond the simple sentence. The young child might write: 'My brother worked as an electrician. He then joined the army.' But this kind of sequence of very basic sentences is tedious. We naturally string the sentences together. Here we might write: 'After working as an electrician, my brother joined the army.' It is often the case that the opening part of a sentence establishes a context or background, positioning the action in some way. It is not surprising, therefore, that these opening words of a sentence are referred to as **introductory or transitional clauses or phrases**. These often locate the action, telling us where, when, why or how the main events took place, at the same time easing the reader into the sentence:

> In the course of colonial history, many crimes have been committed in the name of civilisation.

> After the leaves have fallen from the trees, birds have little cover from the storms.

> If I ruled the world, every day would be the first day of spring.

We also use a comma after introductory words, such as 'Of course' or 'Well': 'Of course, nobody takes Spurs seriously.' To which a loyal Tottenham supporter might reply: 'Well, some of us do.'

Why is a comma required after such introductory or transitional words and phrases? In the case of 'Of course' or 'Well', it simply reflects a natural pause in speaking, but in more complex contexts it clarifies meaning. The very slight pause allows the reader to shift from finding a position to focusing on the real substance of the sentence. Consider this example: 'A kiss on the cheek might be quite continental, but diamonds are a girl's best friend.' This might appear to be an example of the use of the comma described in the previous unit – punctuating linked main clauses. But these two clauses are not quite of equal weight. It is the point about diamonds that is most important. The introductory clause just eases us into the main point.

There is a convention to be grasped here about the use of the comma, but there is also a point that relates to our wider project in this book. The convention of the comma after the introductory material in a sentence is a way of steering the reader along, guiding the reader, pausing and then turning a corner for the reader where necessary. Commas in this sense are just like good manners. Rather than sloppily saying, 'Find your own way through what I've written,' the correct use of punctuation adds precision, clarity and, perhaps most importantly of all, style to what you write. Far too often, students think the ideas are the only things that matter, with language as a kind of wheelbarrow for wheeling ideas along in. But it is the simple gestures of punctuation that enable ideas to come to life.

▶ 34 The six uses of the comma, no. 3: additional and subordinate clauses at the end of sentences

We have just considered the kind of bit that might be inserted at the start of a sentence. It is also the case that an additional bit can be added at the end: 'He was sacked from his job, which came as no surprise to anyone.' This might appear to be the same structure as a compound sentence, with two co-ordinate clauses of equal weight. But the second half of the sentence here ('which came as no surprise to anyone') is an additional or subordinate clause. It adds to the meaning of the main clause, but could not stand on its own as an independent sentence. A comma is used before the subordinate clause in order to clarify the meaning, by making the sentence easier to read.

This might seem a very straightforward use of the comma, but it is in fact one that causes a great deal of confusion. The reason for this is that a lot of sloppy writing relies upon writing down an idea, and then just tagging another idea on to it in a continuation of the sentence. This can lead to the 'comma splice', which we have dealt with in Section 3, and which we will return to again in the next section as it is such a common error in students' writing. Here is another example: 'The rain began to come down heavily, *I was soon wet through.' This is wrong. The problem is that a comma has been used incorrectly to link two separate sentences. We can rectify the problem in three different ways, ways that illustrate the three uses of the comma discussed so far.

We could link the two simple sentences together by using the conjunction 'and': 'The rain began to come down heavily, and I was soon wet through.' This creates a fresh clause with 'and', which in this example requires a comma before it because there is a new subject ('I') in the second clause. We could convert the first half of the sentence into an introductory (adverbial) clause, which means that the real focus of the sentence is 'getting wet through': 'The rain beginning to come down heavily, I was soon wet through.' Again, a comma is needed to signal the change of direction in the sentence. Or we could thrust attention onto the fact of it raining heavily, which would mean that the second half of the sentence would have to become a subordinate clause adding to the meaning of the main clause: 'The rain began to come down heavily, which meant I was soon wet through.' What might come as something of a surprise is the fact that some minor surgery – the addition of a word or two – can turn an error (the comma-spliced sentence) into a correct sentence, and also offer you three stylistic choices about how to present the sentence. That is the real gain of knowing about punctuation: it gives you freedom to add style to your work.

Mistakes in sentences might seem hard to spot if you are a person who habitually makes such mistakes, but speaking the sentence out loud to yourself can often help determine where commas need to appear. This is also true in relation to another very common problem, particularly in the latter stages of a sentence. This is the 'misplaced comma'. Once again this is a case of focusing on the content of writing, and not paying enough attention to how the separate parts of the sentence are being digested by the reader. It would not be uncommon to find a student who wrote: '*The rain began, to come down heavily.' The mistake here is that a comma has been introduced arbitrarily and wrongly, splitting up the verb. The correct versions is: 'The rain began to come down heavily.' It is a case of wanting the punctuation to do too much work; the student wants to emphasise the rain and only then proceed to emphasising its heaviness. But the comma cannot work in this way. It cannot mark off every significant cluster of words in a sentence; it can only separate the separate grammatical units, not the individual parts of a sentence. Above all, it cannot separate the subject and its verb group: '*I, love you' is wrong. A great deal of the logic of commas simply involves noticing that a sentence is reaching the end of a unit of meaning before turning off in a slightly different direction. Reading what you have written out loud to yourself can help you appreciate the location of the natural pauses and changes of direction.

▶ 35 The six uses of the comma, no. 4: subordinate and parenthetical elements within a sentence

Let's take stock. So far we have seen how a comma might appear in a fairly central position in a sentence; if two or more simple sentences are being joined together into one longer sentence a word such as 'and' or 'but' will often be in evidence. Or there might be a comma at an early point in the sentence if there is an introductory phrase or clause before the main clause. In a not dissimilar way, a comma at a late stage in the sentence might signal the introduction of a subordinate, or additional, last clause that supports, by adding to, the meaning of the main clause in the sentence. In all three cases, it is a single comma that is used. But the really impressive effects in writing are created by hammocking extra words or phrases into the body of a sentence. It is this that enables authors to explore ideas in detail, adding nuances, asides and fine distinctions to what they are writing, and to vary the length of their sentences. In these instances, the main point that you need to remember is that commas 'hunt in pairs'.

Whenever there is a parenthetical interpolation in a sentence, you need a comma as the extra unit starts and a comma to signal that it has concluded. This is one of the most common failings in students' essays, that they fail to signal that something is parenthetical. It is an error that reveals itself most often in the use of the word 'however'. The following is wrong: '*There are doubts however, about the authenticity of the painting.' It should be: 'There are doubts, however, about the authenticity of the painting.' It is the same, of course, if you slip a phrase such as 'of course' into a sentence. You do, therefore, need to make yourself aware of the convention. But why is it that when 'however', 'of course' and 'therefore' are inserted in a sentence commas are required before and after? It should, in fact, be obvious by now. If you look at how these parenthetical words and phrases are used in this paragraph, you should be able to see that they are asides, words almost in brackets, that ease the sentence along, establishing a kind of logical and sequential link with what has appeared before and what follows. Of course, if you start a sentence with one of these words or phrases, then it will appear just as it does in this sentence, with a single comma after it.

We have already said that if you can get the commas right in your writing, then most other things will then proceed to fall into place. We would go a step further and suggest that if you can master the rule about 'however' as a parenthetical element inserted in a sentence, and follow the rule in your own writing, then everything else will then fall into place. This will be because you are slowing down the process of dashing off words on a page, and thinking just a little more about how a sentence sounds, pauses and adds little touches that contribute to the main point. (There is one extra refinement. Words like 'however' sometimes follow a semicolon, a point that we deal with in Unit 40. In such cases there is a comma after but not before the word.)

Subordinate clauses within the body of a sentence are treated in the same manner as words such as 'however': 'For many years, the young people of the island, with few if any opportunities for employment, have migrated to the mainland.' In this sentence, there is an adverbial phrase – 'For many years' – and then a main clause: 'the young people of the island have migrated to the mainland'. The subject of this is 'the young people of the island' and the predicate is the fact that they migrate to the mainland. But there is an additional piece of information – 'with few if any opportunities for employment' – which could have appeared as the next sentence: 'This is because there are few if any opportunities for employment.' But too many simple sentences would seem to labour the point; the additional information can, therefore, be elegantly interpolated into the sentence as a subordinate clause.

But you must remember to signal this with an opening and closing comma or there will be cases where the meaning is far from clear. In this instance, if we missed out the commas the sentence would read: 'For many years, the young people of the island with few if any opportunities for employment have migrated to the mainland.' The subject of the sentence is now 'the young people of the island with few if any opportunities for employment'. The meaning of the sentence in this revised form is that only those who couldn't find work left, whereas in the first instance it meant that all the young people left. We might seem to be making a great deal of fuss about something very trivial, but it is sloppiness about punctuation details that limits the ability of many students to say what they really want to say in an essay. In order to convey what you want to convey, you don't need to be a genius; you simply need to follow the very, very simple rules about the placing of commas.

▶ 36 The six uses of the comma, no. 5: appositives

Most people have never come across the word 'apposition'. It would seem a reasonable guess that it must have some connection with the idea of 'opposition', and in a sense this is true, but there is not the same idea of conflict involved. It is closer to an idea of simply being along-side. More technically, apposition is a grammatical construction in which two or more nouns (or noun phrases) are put together without being linked by 'and', 'but', 'or' etc. An appositive is a word or phrase that follows a noun to identify, define or rename it. We use these all the time in writing and speaking, but in writing you must remember to include the comma as you start the identifying, defining or renaming, and you must remember to include the comma as your identifying, defining or renaming ends.

> Victoria Beckham, formerly known as Posh Spice, was among the guests.
> Robbie Williams, Britain's leading male recording artist, was there too.
> Will Young, the most successful Pop Idol winner, arrived a little after ten.

Sometimes the distinction between an appositive and a subordinate or parenthetical clause within a sentence might not be entirely clear to you as you write, for example, the following: 'Elton John, stunningly dressed in a pink and lime suit, performed at the piano.' You might not be sure whether 'stunningly dressed in a pink and lime suit' is in apposition (because it identifies Elton a little more closely) or whether it is an adjectival phrase. But being able to stick a label on the construction is far less important than recognising that there is a simple sentence – 'Elton John [subject] performed [verb] at the piano [complement]' – and that, because some extra information has been popped into the sentence, this has to be signalled by commas.

More specifically, this has to be signalled by the kind of commas that 'hunt in pairs'. It is the same if we write: 'Robbie Williams, who can always be relied upon to make everyone smile, sang a song from his new album.' As is so often the case with commas, just the normal pauses that characterise our speech patterns – the fact that we would pause momentarily after 'Williams' and after 'smile' – can help us iden-tify where the commas should appear. But there should also be a way in which your eye runs over a sentence that you have put together, seeing whether everything seems in order. The more confident one becomes as a writer, the more one acquires an 'eye' for detecting an error. But even the most experienced writers often have to sort out and identify their core sentence (the subject/verb/complement or **object sequence**) before they can be sure that everything else has been slotted in and added correctly. What we are saying is that, if even professional writers are quite happy to check the basics, there is every-thing to be said for other writers making the same kind of checks.

▶ 37 The six uses of the comma, no. 6: commas between items in a series, and between two or more adjectives that equally modify the same word

Commas are used to separate the items in a series or list: 'There are hamburgers, sausages, chips, peas, ice cream and lollipops in our freezer.' There is always a logic that informs the use of commas, so what is the logic that underlies the use of commas in a list or series? As always, where we pause, even momentarily, in reading the sentence determines where commas could and should appear. But what we can also see is that a sentence might look silly if the commas were omitted in a list: 'Those nursing injuries in the first team squad are Gary Stevens Gary Smith Gerald Peters Peter Gerald Gianlucca Mazarini and William Prince.' The words begin to swim in front of the reader's eyes in the unpunctuated version of this sentence. Add the commas and everything acquires shape and meaning: 'Those nursing injuries in the first team squad are Gary Stevens, Gary Smith, Gerald Peters, Peter Gerald, Gianlucca Mazarini and William Prince.'

In Britain it is standard practice not to use a comma before the co-ordinating conjunction 'and' in a list. Americans, however, tend to use a comma in this context, and some older grammar books insist that there is no justification for missing out the comma before the 'and', as there is just the same pause as at every other stage in the sentence. But the fact is that most people in Britain today don't use the final comma, unless it is necessary in order to make the meaning clear. Consider the difference between these two sentences:

> The table was piled high with food: cakes, jam, bread and butter.

> I checked my shopping list: cakes, jam, bread, and butter.

A comma has been slipped into the second sentence just to make it clear that I am intending to buy two items – some bread and some butter – rather than some ready-buttered bread. Of course, you might say, don't be silly; shops don't sell ready-buttered bread. And nine times out of ten there would be no possibility of confusion, but if there is the slightest possibility of confusion, then there is a lot to be said for being pedantically accurate in your use of punctuation.

In a rather similar way to commas separating the items in a list, a comma is normally inserted between two adjectives limiting (that is to say, describing) the same noun and preceding it.

It was a long, dark tunnel.
She was a young, innocent girl.

He was a cold-blooded, psychopathic murderer.

Fortunately, she stayed at home that night, washing her long, fair hair.

There is a comma between the two adjectives, but don't make the mistake of adding an extra, unnecessary comma after the second adjective and before the noun. Sometimes a comma between the two adjectives is incorrect. This is where the second adjective is so closely associated with the noun that in a sense the adjective and noun together constitute a noun phrase. For example, we might write 'She was a little old lady.' We could write 'She was a little, old lady.' There is a difference in meaning. Imagine the police had asked you if you had seen an old lady. You might answer: 'Yes, she was a little old lady.' But you would pause in a different place if they asked you if you had seen a lady, 'Yes, she was a little, old lady.' As with so many things concerning commas, everything becomes apparent – most specifically where the commas need to appear – if you read the sentence out loud to yourself, noting where, if even for a thousandth of a second, you pause for breath.

The six uses of the comma: examples and explanations

1. *Punctuating linked main clauses*

'Society depends on its traditions, and the authority of the written text is one of these.'

2. *Setting off the introductory element of a sentence*

As in this sentence, we need to look at this common use of the comma. It can be considered as the introductory or transitional phrase that sets up a sentence: 'In the course of the nineteenth century, attitudes towards religious belief changed considerably.' 'After the collapse of communism, Russia was thrown into turmoil.' 'Ultimately, we are all doomed.'

3. *Additional and subordinate clauses at the end of sentences*

'The validity of the written word is an old belief that people hang on to, ignoring the world as it changes around them.'

➔➔➔

4. Subordinating and parenthetical elements within a sentence

This is one of the most common mistakes in students' essays. When you pop a word such as 'however' or 'therefore' into a sentence, it is a parenthetical element, intended to ease things along. It is essential, therefore, that a comma appears before and after the word. Far too many students leave out both the commas, or just include one after the word: '*It is wrong however, to do this.' This last sentence should read: 'It is wrong, however, to do this.'
It is, however, not just parenthetical phrases that are inserted in sentences. There are also subordinate clauses, which might be regarded as non-essential material in a sentence. They are, of course, only non-essential in the sense that the sentence would still make sense even if they were removed. If you are writing an essay, such clauses add nuances and shades of meaning to your work, as in this example: 'The farming references in Hardy's novel, so often the point of contact between humanity and nature, suggest the precariousness of rural existence.'

5. Appositives

This is a phrase or noun that renames another noun: 'Hardy's final novel, *Jude the Obscure*, is dark and gloomy.' Can you see why that sentence requires commas whereas the following sentence does not? 'Hardy's novel *Jude the Obscure* is dark and gloomy.' In the second example, the novel is not being renamed; on the contrary, which Hardy novel is being referred to is not apparent until the title has been given.

6. Commas between items in a series, and between two or more adjectives that equally modify the same word

Americans tend to write: 'Breakfast consisted of bacon, egg, and fried bread.' In Britain we would usually write: 'Breakfast consisted of bacon, egg and fried bread.' We might include the final comma if it clarified the meaning. 'I looked at Martin's old, haggard face.' Both these adjectives equally modify the noun. We do not use a comma if the adjective next to the noun is closer to the noun in meaning. 'Nothing has quite as much potential to surprise us as the Victorian realistic novel.'

▶ 38 Moments of doubt and hesitation: do I need a comma?

A lot of the time, students fail to include commas when they need to be included in a sentence. Sometimes, however, the use of a comma is optional. The opening sentence of this unit, for example, can appear as: 'A lot of the time students fail to include commas when they need to be included in a sentence.' It could be argued that after the opening phrase in the sentence any pause for breath is so infinitesimal that a comma would simply be fussy. But it is also easy to see that 'A lot of the time' is a group of words that makes sense as a unit of meaning and so can be read with a pause after them. It is, obviously, sometimes hard to know where to include a comma and where it can safely be missed out. Perhaps the best advice we can offer is to remember the distinction between commas that appear on their own, to mark off the opening or closing bits of a sentence, and the commas that 'hunt in pairs': the commas that 'hunt in pairs' always signal some parenthetical element that has been introduced into the sentence, and the start and conclusion of such an interpolation must always be signalled to the reader.

In the next section we will turn to some common mistakes with commas: there is the comma splice, which we have already touched on, but which needs to be returned to again and again. And there is also a very common student error of slipping in a comma for no reason at all after the noun or noun phrase that constitutes the subject element of a sentence has been completed. But, for the moment, we want to turn to two rather more substantial punctuation marks than the comma: the colon [:] and the semicolon [;]. What we mean by 'more substantial' is not that they are more important than commas – indeed, there is nothing quite as important as the comma in generating good writing – but that they represent a rather more substantial pause for breath than the comma.

▶ 39 Convincing use of the colon

What an odd word 'colon' is! Isn't the colon something to do with people's bottoms? But that is beside the point. There are three things to remember about colons:

1. Colons introduce a list, set up a quotation or definition, or they might precede a series of clauses.
2. Students often use a colon where they should be using a semi-colon. (One reason for this is that the semicolon now does the kind of work done by a colon in books written in the nineteenth century.)
3. If in doubt, find a way of not using either the colon or the semi-colon.

Here are examples of the use of a colon.

> She tipped out the contents of her handbag: keys, a credit card, lipstick, cigarettes, a lighter, fifty thousand pounds in used notes and a Colt 45 automatic revolver.

> He reflected on the words of his Chief Inspector: never judge by appearances.

> With an air of satisfaction, he reflected on his day: he had arrested an innocent-looking nun; she had sung like a canary; her handbag had contained damning evidence; she had incriminated the entire convent; he would be home in time to put the kids to bed.

Don't make the common mistake of thinking you can pick up a sentence again after the colon. What we mean by this is that students often use it correctly to set up a list, but then try to continue with the meaning of the first part of the sentence after the colon and the material that it has set up. This is wrong:

> George Eliot then produced her finest novels: *The Mill on the Floss*, *Middlemarch* and *Daniel Deronda*, *the last of which focuses most alarmingly on the woman's fate in life.

Why this is wrong is that the colon can only set up what immediately relates to it. After the list, or whatever, has been completed, a fresh sentence is required:

> George Eliot then produced her finest novels: *The Mill on the Floss*, *Middlemarch* and *Daniel Deronda*. It is the last of these that focuses most alarmingly on the woman's fate in life.

▶ 40 Stylish use of the semicolon

We imagine that most readers of this book know what a semicolon is. But it is a reasonable bet that almost as many are not entirely sure when and where they can legitimately use a semicolon. The first thing that we want to stress, therefore, is that it is perfectly possible to be a good writer without ever using a semicolon. It is a kind of refined piece of weaponry in your punctuation armoury, something that adds an extra touch of sophistication to writing, but which is never absolutely necessary and which you need never produce at all. Indeed, one of the authors of this book completed an undergraduate degree and then a postgraduate degree without ever using semicolons, simply because, at that time, he didn't know how to use them. Now that he has learned how to use them, he uses them so often – in a rather pathetic, 'look at me I know how to use semicolons' way – that it would probably be a good idea if he forgot how to use them. This is because the use of semi-colons should be sparing and calculated.

But that is something we will turn to in a moment. Let's sort out the basic principles first. The significance of the semicolon begins to become apparent if we think about it as a written sign. It is actually a rather odd-looking sign [;], but the oddness of its appearance defines its function. It is more than a comma, because we put a stop over the comma, but less than a full stop, because we put a comma under the stop. Wherever we use a semicolon, we could simply use a full stop. But sometimes, to vary the pattern of sentences, and to add an extra degree of emphasis and impact, we can insert a semicolon between what we were going to write as two sentences. The circumstances in which we can do this are if the two potential sentences contain ideas that are closely linked; the use of the semicolon pulls the two units of thought more closely together.

We could write: 'He had been away from his family for six months. It was a hard and depressing existence.' But it adds a degree of impact to the two sentences if we choose to emphasise how one idea more or less overlaps with or is closely related to the other: 'He had been away from his family for six months; it was a hard and depressing existence.' This only really works, however, if the use of such an effect is sparing. The following does not work as an effective piece of writing:

> He had been away from his family for six months; it was a hard and depressing existence. Once a week, two of the men struggled down to the base camp; they would return tired and dispirited. Fresh rations had not been sent; indeed, it was becoming apparent that they would never be sent. Then, one night, Jones quietly slipped into a coma and died; it was the fate that conceivably awaited them all.

This doesn't work as a piece of writing because the pattern is mechanically repetitive; each sentence has more or less the same structure, so each sentence makes less and less of an impact.

This is how we would be inclined to rewrite that paragraph. Our starting point is one that we have stressed throughout this book: start with a simple, bold sentence.

> He had been away from his family for six months. It was a hard and depressing existence. Once a week, two of the men struggled down to the base camp, but they would return tired and dispirited. Fresh rations had not been sent, and, indeed, it was becoming apparent that they would never be sent. Then, one night, Jones quietly slipped into a coma and died; it was the fate that conceivably awaited them all.

We have used simple sentences, then compound sentences (relying on 'but' and 'and'), but have deliberately saved the semicolon for the end of the paragraph. This is a good stylistic trick. By joining together the last two statements in a paragraph (if you feel that you can legitimately do so) you create an impressive rhetorical effect of seeming to tie together everything that you have said so far. This is probably the best way of thinking about the semicolon: it pulls two sentences together, and is best used as a rhetorical effect at those points in an essay where you want to synthesise your ideas up to that point. The semicolon, in a rather clever, almost sneaky, way, manages to make connections that are not being explicitly expressed in what you have written. On the contrary, rather than a connection being explicitly suggested to your audience, the reader is put in a position where two separate units of thought are being nudged together into a relationship. If you can see the logic, and usefulness, of that, you are starting to grasp one of the advanced secrets of effective writing: that there is a level beyond just saying what you have to say in an efficient manner, which is using words (and punctuation) craftily to control the response of your reader, almost invisibly.

5 Avoidable Errors

▶ **41 If it looks wrong and sounds wrong, it probably is wrong**

Writing is like driving a car. It's relatively easy, but a lot of people write carelessly, even recklessly. Let us assume for the moment, however, that you have negotiated the fundamentals: you can steer a sentence along, stopping, with a full stop, when you need to stop, and changing gear, in the sense of introducing a comma, when you have to turn a corner, change speed or make an adjustment in a sentence. With a little bit of practice and particularly if you think about what you are doing as you proceed, you will find yourself in control of these basic manoeuvres.

But even if you are progressing in a fairly steady manner, there is another problem to be aware of in writing. A lot of what people write is blighted by silly little errors in sentence after sentence. Consider the following. They are sentences from the opening paragraphs of essays by university students.

(i)   Poverty in the developing world has effected the lives of millions of its' inhabitants.

(ii) Is it a remedy that could prove off importance.

(iii) These different views suggests a tension in our societies values.

(iv) This description fails to do justice to the charitable work undertook by many, during these years.

What are the errors here? Well, we aren't going to go into them in detail at this stage, but they are:

using the wrong word
an incorrectly used apostrophe
failing to put a question mark at the end of a sentence
failure to match plural with plural (the technical term is 'agreement')
confusion about the correct form of a singular noun
using the wrong tense of a verb
a misplaced comma that destroys the sense of a sentence.

See if you can work out why these are the correct versions of the sentences above:

(i)   Poverty in the developing world has affected the lives of millions of its inhabitants.
(ii)   Is it a remedy that could prove of importance?
(iii)   These different views suggest a tension in our society's values.
(iv)   This description fails to do justice to the charitable work undertaken by many during these years.

If you cannot see what the mistakes were in the original sentences, keep reading this unit, and then the section as a whole.

It doesn't matter if you make a few errors when you are writing. Even the best writers make the occasional blunder. But the fact is that some students make very few mistakes in essays whereas other students make them over and over, with mistakes littering every sentence. The answer to the problem starts with reading your work out loud to yourself, though there are also other ways of doing this. There is a method called 'sub-vocalising', where you sound the words in your head. If you do that it should help you to identify things that sound wrong. In the rest of this section, we want to focus on the typical errors that creep into essays again and again. If you don't take care over such details, you give out the wrong signals about your work: either that you don't know or, even worse, that you don't care.

But what were the errors? In sentence (i), the correct word is 'affected', not 'effected', and it is wrong to use an apostrophe after 'its'. In sentence (ii), the correct word is 'of', not 'off', and the question mark is missing at the end of the sentence. In sentence (iii), there is confusion about singular and plural (it should be 'suggest', not 'suggests'), and the writer fails to use the singular form 'society's'. In sentence (iv), the tense is wrong (it should be 'undertaken', not 'undertook'), and the comma is unnecessary.

▶ 42 Make sure you are using a word that exists, and make sure you are using the right word

It sometimes happens that in straining to say what they want to say students create words that they think, perhaps hope, will serve the required function in a sentence. '*There are problems with the resocietalisation of long-term prisoners.' What we think the student is trying to say is that people leaving prison find it difficult adjusting to their new lives, but the long word she uses is not actually a word and, even if it were a word, it sounds ugly. The problem occurs because it often proves difficult finding the words to say what one wants to say, but another aspect is the desire to sound weighty and sophisticated. The student makes a pretentious attempt to impress, hoping that a long word will carry more clout than a simple word. But this is never the case.

So what is the remedy? If you have written something that, on reflection, strikes you as sounding ugly or just plain wrong, then the probability is that it is wrong. The answer is to reconstruct the sentence, trying to express the idea as plainly as possible. You won't go far wrong if you try to convey the idea in words that an eleven-year-old would understand. In the example above, for example, you could say 'On their release, long-term prisoners find it difficult readjusting to society.' This issue of the wrong word, the over-ambitious word or the word that just doesn't sound right, is a common one in students' work. The answer is the answer that underlies everything we are saying in this book: keep it simple. If a sentence feels wrong because you suspect one or more of the words is wrong, you must set about reconstructing the sentence – simplifying it in accordance with the simple rules of sentence construction so that it says what it actually needs to say. In the example above, the sentence has been reconstructed with a simpler subject/predicate pattern:

> On their release [**introductory phrase**], long-term prisoners [**subject**] find [**verb**] it [**object**] difficult readjusting to society [**complement**].

The point we are making is that an implicit awareness of the standard pattern of a sentence has enabled us to disentangle and rephrase the sentence so that it now says clearly what the student wanted to say.

This principle of keeping things simple should help you avoid ugliness of expression and extreme mistakes with individual words. Even more common, however, is the problem of students not knowing the difference between two words – and always managing to use the wrong one. The error that appears most often in students' essays is not knowing the difference between 'effect' and 'affect'. Other problem words are 'principle' and 'principal', 'complement' and 'compliment', and 'their' and 'there'. You have to know the difference between 'their' and 'there'; the words are used so often that you can't often write a paragraph without using one or the other. But if you are unsure about the others, consult a dictionary, find a different word or reconstruct the sentence. Above all, don't get them wrong in your university or job application.

Sometimes a mistake occurs because the writer has failed to modify the word in the correct way when the context demands a modification. You must always take care over words that end in *y* in the singular and *ies* in the plural, such as 'society/societies' and 'country/countries'. If you are talking about Britain, for example, make sure it is the singular form that you use.

> The country's exports rose steeply.

But it is different if you are talking about more than one country.

> The countries of Eastern Europe are keen to join the European Union.

'Countries' here is, of course, the plural form of 'country'. It is a simple distinction, and easy to grasp, but you wouldn't believe how many people fail to use the correct singular form of such words when adding an apostrophe s. Getting something like this wrong is terribly embarrassing, but it only takes a moment's thought to get it right.

▶ 43 Slang in a sentence and too many words in a sentence

Sometimes it is individual words in a sentence that grate. At other times it is a sentence as a whole, which might say what the writer is trying to say but in a manner that is too informal. The problem here is a failure to distinguish between the spoken word and the written word. Speech is very casual; we keep on adding words and phrases to clarify and reinforce what we want to say. But sentences in a piece of written work cannot proliferate in the same way. Consider this: 'This is a reason as to why the economy collapsed so rapidly.' The words 'a reason as to why' might be something that we could get away with in conversation, but that is the problem with the words. The phrase is too colloquial, too much like slang.

If you find yourself writing something like this – and reading your essay back to yourself, sub-vocalising it, should reveal whether there is a problem – you need to tinker with the sentence. If you do not spot the error initially, there is always another stage in checking your work, where you should be going through each sentence, examining whether improvements can be made and, more specifically, seeing what words can be cut. At that stage you might realise that it would be more correct, more elegant and more effective to write: 'This is one reason why the economy collapsed so rapidly.' What we are referring to here is the problem of sloppy writing. The answer is to look at the sentence and ask whether the subject/verb/complement progression is being achieved in the simplest and most direct terms.

A related problem occurs when students change their ideas as they are writing a sentence, but then fail to return to examine the sequence of words they have written. They have failed to cast a reflective eye over what is being said. The result, time and time again, is that the sentence includes a few stray or additional words: '*In order to do this she needs to purge herself from of the toxins that are poisoning her system.' The problem here is casting around for the correct word, wavering between 'from' and 'of', and then including both. The sentence should read: 'In order to do this she needs to purge herself of the toxins that are poisoning her system.' If the sentence had been read out loud, the student would probably have spotted the mistake.

You might, of course, think that the kind of problem we are discussing here is something that happens very rarely, but this is not the case. Alongside problems with punctuation, it is a lack of care in writing – the proliferation of extra words, a sequence of words that doesn't quite read as correct English should read, and a general slackness about expression – that is the most common problem in the work of school, college and university students. The problem starts because the student is struggling hard to express an idea. Sometimes, the resulting sentences become so elaborate that they get entirely snarled up. This is from an essay by a student training to be a doctor: '*The pain, which that have affected her life disablingly previously to this, should by the end of the period during which treatment is being received to her will hopefully have alleviated in some extent.' Now, it might well be that you feel you are never going to write a sentence as faulty as that. But the fact is that most students at some stage at school, college or university will write sentences that go wrong in at least some of the ways that this sentence goes wrong.

What is the answer? If you have read your work out loud to yourself, you should have reached the point where you are aware when something needs a touch of corrective surgery: 'By the end of the period of treatment, her disabling pain should be alleviated to some extent.' Or: 'Her disabling pain should, by the end of the period of treatment, be alleviated to some extent.' As always, the answer to sorting out a sentence is to identify the core of what is being said, which means recognising the subject and predicate (the verb and complement) pattern of the sentence. This student's muddle could have been sorted out by recognising that the subject is 'her disabling pain', the verb is that something 'should' happen and the complement is that it will be 'alleviated to some extent'. The temporal phrase 'by the end of the period of treatment' can then be slotted into the sentence in either of two positions, with commas signalling that it is a supporting clause. Or it could go at the end: 'Her disabling pain should be alleviated to some extent by the end of the period of treatment.' This gives a straightforward subject/verb/complement order. All messy, over-complicated and embarrassingly badly written sentences can be sorted out in this way: identify the main thing that is being said, and then slot in a subsidiary clause or phrase as required.

▶ **44 Agreement**

Many of the slips and errors we are looking at are very minor, but the impact they have is often quite considerable. Such is the case with 'agreement'. By this we mean that the subject and verb in a sentence must agree or match: if there is a singular subject, then the verb must also be singular; if the subject is plural (that is, more than one), then the verb must be plural. It would be incorrect, for example, if we had started this paragraph as follows: '*Many of the slips and errors we is looking at is very minor, but the impact they has is quite considerable.' There are two errors here: we need the plural verb form 'are' to agree with the plural word 'we' ('we are'), and we need the plural verb form 'have' rather than the singular form 'has' to go with the plural word 'they'. The sentence, then, should read: 'Many of the slips and errors we are looking at are very minor, but the impact they have is quite considerable.'

Let's take a further look at an example of the same problem. If someone were to say 'I are a farmer', you would immediately notice that the person has said 'I are' instead of 'I am'. He or she has used the plural form of the verb – 'are' – which normally goes with the plural words 'we', 'you' or 'they'. Rather than using standard English, they are using a non-standard or dialect form. There are, of course, different varieties of English. Standard English – which is what this book is about – is not any better than, say, dialect. It is, however, the form that by convention we use when we write.

This is an important point to bear in mind. The rules about 'correct' English, specifically written English, are arbitrary conventions. There is nothing wrong with saying 'I are a farmer'. Millions of people use similar constructions in their everyday speech; they use, that is, forms such as 'I ain't done nothing'. But confusion could ensue if someone was attempting to communicate with another person who operated in accordance with another convention. Again, if the farmer wrote to his bank saying 'I are a farmer and I'd like it if you could lend me money for a couple of fields I are considering buying', the bank manager, in a world where bank managers no longer know their customers personally, might assume that the farmer doesn't seem like a very sound applicant for a loan. This is because business is conducted through Standard English: it is the standard way of communicating in education, law and government. It is used, along with its so-called rules, so that people can communicate in a way they both understand, and in a way where the manner of saying something helps rather than hinders what is being said.

Fortunately, the rules are simplicity itself. We will see this if we return to the opening examples of errors in this section (Unit 41) and look at number (iii):

These different views suggests a tension in our societies values.

There are two errors here. One is an error to do with the apostrophe – it should be 'society's values', not 'societies values' – which we look at in the next section. The other error is an error of agreement. The student has written '*These different views suggests a tension in our societies values,' but should have written 'These different views suggest a tension in our society's values.' The subject of the sentence, 'These different views', is plural, and so the verb also needs to be in the plural form: 'suggest'. Subject and verb, then, need to agree: if one is plural, the other also has to be plural.

But how do you know what a plural verb is? The answer is that you do not have to know. English is in fact a very simple language where most verbs stay the same regardless of whether the subject is singular or plural. It makes no difference if we write 'I love' or 'we love' or 'you love television'. The verb 'love' stays the same. This is also true of the past tense: 'I walked there'; 'you walked there'; 'we walked there'; 'they walked there'; 'she walked there'. In each case the verb 'walked' is identical; we only know the sentence is plural because the subject – 'I' or 'we' – tells us. In effect, there is no verb form for the plural.

There is just one point at which difference matters, and this student has stumbled across it. This is in the present tense when we are talking about a third person: 'I love', but 'she loves'. We add an *s* here to the verb form 'love'; so, too, with 'walk': 'she walks'. It is ironic that the only place where the verb can change is the place where students most often slip up, usually by wrongly adding an *s*, as the student does above: 'These different views suggest'. Sometimes, however, students leave the *s* off. They leave it off when it is needed, writing 'he like me', instead of 'he likes me'. Of course, it may be that the student has dashed the sentence off and not noticed the slip, but it might also be the case that the student simply does not know the difference between singular (one) and plural (many) and so cannot easily spot errors. If you are prone to slips, getting to the root of errors such as this can be very productive for your writing.

Here there is good evidence that the student is not quite sure of the system of singular and plural. That evidence is in the word 'societies'. This means several 'societies'; it is the plural form of the word 'society'. The student has come across the word societies or heard it, but doesn't know that it is the plural of 'society'. He or she thinks it is another word: 'society's'. A great deal of confusion in writing stems from this basic point of not knowing that words do change when they become plural:

city	→	cities
sky	→	skies
baby	→	babies

Millions of words add *s* to make them plural, but a large number change *y* to *ies* to become plural.

Agreement is about making sure that the subjects and the verbs of your sentences match. But behind this idea lies the larger, simpler, point of recognising the difference between singular and plural. Many of the mistakes in essays and everyday writing stem from the failure to grasp this basic point. It is not helped by the way in which English as a language sometimes appears to have some odd plurals – 'foot' becomes 'feet', 'child' becomes 'children' – but in general the plural is marked by an *s* or an *es* ('fish' – 'fishes'). Once you have that point secure, then a lot of other problems can be worked out because you know everything must agree: singular with singular, plural with plural.

We have said that there is only one point at which verbs change – the third person present tense. This, however, is not true of the verb 'to be', which seems to break all the rules:

I am; you are; she is

we are; you are; they are.

You might be mystified as to why we have included 'you are' twice here. The first 'you are' is the singular form, when we are talking to one other person; the second 'you are' is identical but here is meant to indicate that we are talking to several other people. In many languages these two forms of 'you' have different words, but in English they are the same.

Underlying this rather odd point is something very important. We learn most of the usual rules about language as children. One of the main rules we learn is that of agreement; we learn, that is, how verbs match the person: 'I am', 'you are', 'she is'; 'I run'; 'she runs', 'they run'. 'Person' here is the 'I', 'you', 'she' 'they' bits. It is a technical term, indicating different people; it helps us distinguish between the speaker ('I') or the first person; the person spoken to ('you'), also known as the 'addressee' or the second person; and the third party ('she', 'he', and 'it'), or the third person. We can list these three categories:

first person: I
second person: you
third person: he, she, it

These are the singular forms. The following are the plural forms:

first person plural: we
second person plural: you
third person plural: they

We call these words 'I', 'you', 'she' personal pronouns. Understanding this set of terms is not crucial to writing a good essay. It is, however, enormously helpful if you do know your way around the basics of grammar: that subject and verb agree, and that there are singular and plural forms of most nouns and pronouns. A great deal falls into place once these simple points are known. Just as important, once you have singular and plural firmly fixed, the problem of the apostrophe, the subject of the next section, will begin to dwindle; it will seem that we are doing little more than stating the obvious.

▶ 45 Apostrophes

> *My Saturday job is in Marks and Spencers' busiest shop.
>
> *My Saturday job is in Tescos busiest supermarket.
>
> *My Saturday job is selling hamburger's.
>
> *My Saturday job is looking after my uncle Jame's dog.

All four of these sentences are incorrect: the first has the apostrophe in the wrong place, the second needs an apostrophe, the third shouldn't have an apostrophe, and the fourth also has the apostrophe in the wrong place. Students make so many mistakes with apostrophes that we could suggest that the best answer to the problem would be to do the opposite of what you first feel inclined to do: if you think an apostrophe should be included, the chances are that it shouldn't! But such frivolous advice isn't all that much help if you don't actually know what an apostrophe is. And, moreover, the rules concerning the apostrophe are so easy to master that it is worth making the effort and learning them. Misplaced or missing apostrophes are one of the things that people are judged on in all kinds of situations in life. If you get them wrong, people dismiss you as unsatisfactory. If you get them right, people assume that you are super-intelligent.

First of all, let's sort out the sentences above, remembering that we use the apostrophe with an s to show something belongs to someone:

> My Saturday job is in Marks and Spencer's busiest shop.
>
> My Saturday job is in Tesco's busiest supermarket.
>
> My Saturday job is selling hamburgers.
>
> My Saturday job is looking after my uncle James's dog.

The logic here is quite simple: in the first sentence the name of the company is Marks and Spencer, so the apostrophe comes before the *s*: it means 'my Saturday job is in the busiest shop belonging to Marks and Spencer.' (It doesn't matter that the sign over the door of the shop you work in says 'Woolworths', or perhaps something like 'Woolworths Local'. Shops often prefer to display their name without the apostrophe. In the same way, you will come across 'Boots', even though the founder of the company was called Mr Boot and so, strictly speaking, it should be Boot's.) In the second sentence, the name of the company is Tesco, so this time the apostrophe again comes before the *s*. In the third sentence there is no apostrophe: 'my job is to sell hamburgers', which is the plural of the noun 'hamburger'. In the fourth sentence, we need to see that my job is looking after the dog belonging to my uncle James. What, therefore, we need to write is 'James's dog': the apostrophe comes after the s here because his name is James, not Jame.

The apostrophe causes more daily chaos than broken traffic lights: everywhere you go you see *potato's* for sale or *used cars'*, not to mention *TV's'*. The first thing to learn about the apostrophe is that it has nothing to do with making words plural. The plural of 'potato' is 'potatoes', of 'tomato' it is 'tomatoes', of 'TV' it is 'televisions'! We make words plural in the main by adding s. That's it. When we use the apostrophe we mean that something belongs to somebody. This use of the apostrophe is called the **possessive**, meaning 'belonging to'. In 'the girl's car' the word 'girl's' shows ownership: the car belongs to the girl. Wherever there is a possessive it can nearly always be translated to mean 'belonging to': 'the dog's tail' means 'the tail belonging to the dog'; 'the woman's phone' means 'the phone belonging to the woman'.

There is a slower (and really boring) method of sorting out the apostrophe. It is slow, but it has its uses if you want to sort out what seems to be a problem or muddle in something you have written. We have to admit, however, that the next few paragraphs might be more confusing than helpful. If you are still unsure what is meant by 'the girl's car', translate the phrase this way: take 'the girl's car', move the word 'girl's' after the word 'car' so that you have 'the car girl's', and then translate 'girl's' into 'of the girl'. This might seem very cumbersome but it works. The only word you move is 'girl's'; then you change 'girl's' into 'of the girl'. The trick here is to see that everything before the apostrophe in the word 'girl's' stays the same; the apostrophe and everything after it is turned into the words 'of the'. In effect, you translate the apostrophe s into 'of the'.

This is all very fine, you might feel, with simple words like 'girl', but what happens if it is 'the boss's car'? Exactly the same: 'the boss's car' becomes 'the car (boss's) of the boss'. What happens with plural words? If we are talking about 'the men's actions', how does that translate? Once more it's easy: 'the actions (men's) of the men'. In each case, the basic part of the word remains the same – boss, men – and in each case the **apostrophe s** becomes 'of the'.

How can this trick help you spot if you made a mistake or help if you want to check your work? Let's go back to the example in the previous unit: 'These different views suggests a tension in our socieities values.'

The student should have written 'These different views suggest a tension in our society's values.' We have sorted out the problem of the verb 'suggests' and hope that you now know why it has to be 'suggest'. But what about the second problem here, 'our societies values'? We have noted that the word 'societies' is the plural of the noun 'society' and that what the student should write is 'society's'. Our usual advice has been to sound things out in order to correct them, but here is a case where it will not help to vocalise the words: 'society's' and 'societies' sound exactly the same. This, of course, is why the student has made the error. The student knows, in some vague way, that what is needed here is the possessive form but can't quite manage to see what that might be.

The way to check is to follow the translation method. We start with 'our societies values', and then move the words 'our societies' to the end of the phrase: 'values our societies'. Secondly, we then change the apostrophe and everything after it into 'of the'. Clearly we can't do this since there is no apostrophe. Something, therefore, must be wrong: the apostrophe has been wrongly omitted. The natural instinct is to put it in at the end, thus: 'our societies' values'. Technically, this is grammatically correct. But what does it mean? It means this: 'the values of our societies'. Everything before the apostrophe, remember, stays the same when you translate: 'the values (our societies') of our societies'.

It could conceivably be the case that the writer really did mean to say that there is a tension in the values of our various societies throughout the world, but the chances are that what the student wanted to argue was that there is a tension in the values of our society. In other words he or she wanted to write about society (singular), not about the whole set of societies that make up the world: 'These different views suggest a tension in our society's values.' Once again, the way to check this for yourself is to translate it: 'These different views suggest a tension in the values (our society's) of our society.'

In many cases, you can simply avoid the apostrophe by rephrasing what you want to say. Our student could very easily have written 'These different views suggest a tension in the values of our society.' This is perfectly correct and clear. Avoiding the apostrophe is not, after all, a crime. There is, however, something pathetic about running away from a little mark like the apostrophe.

▶ 46 Its and it's

When someone has a toothache, they are always rather surprised that such a small problem can cause so much pain and irritation. In a similar way, it is always surprising what a nuisance a word as small as 'its' can be. As university teachers, we don't think we have got through a single day without seeing mistakes in the use of 'its'. And it is all the more surprising as there is really no difficulty at all about using the word correctly. Even if you get it wrong, there is an immediate, totally straightforward check that you can make to see whether a correction needs to be made.

'The newspaper apologised for its mistake.' This is the standard usage. You must think of any other form as a variant that you hesitate for a moment before using. But what other form? There is only one variant: 'It's my party, and I'll cry if I want to.' There is no such form as its', where an apostrophe is placed after the *s*. There are three things that you have to tell yourself if you are in doubt:

- Your first instinct should be to write **its**.
- **It's** is an abbreviation of **it is**. Sub-vocalise what you have written. Are you really saying 'it is'? If you are, it can be **it's** in what you are writing.
- But an essay is a formal exercise. There is, therefore, really no place in an essay for a contraction such as **it's** (just as you should not use 'can't' or 'don't' in an essay). If you are writing an essay, it will either be **its** or **it is** that is appropriate.

The difference between **its** and **it's**, then, is that **it's** is a contraction. The apostrophe signals that two words have been contracted into one, and that a letter has been omitted. It is usually a contraction of 'it is', but can be a contraction of 'it has' as in: 'It's been one hell of a day.'

As we say, contractions are best avoided in a formal essay, but sometimes what you are writing will sound too stiff and fussy if you avoid all use of this contraction. *It's* for you to decide if *it's* appropriate to use the less formal variant. (You might well have noticed that we have opted for an informal style in this book, using constructions such as 'doesn't' rather than 'does not'; some readers will object to this, but it seemed the best way of making a book that deals with points of grammar a little more user-friendly.) But the fact remains that the only way to check the accuracy of what you have written is to speak the words back to yourself. It sounds correct if we say: *It is* for you to decide if *it is* appropriate to use the less formal variant. But the sentence 'The newspaper apologised for its mistake,' cannot be changed to '*The newspaper apologised for it is mistake.' As with so many things, all that is required is a moment's reflection. English spelling is often odd, but everything else – such as the difference between **its** and **it's** – functions in accordance with very simple rules.

▶ 47 Punctuation blunders: the comma splice again

There are some points that we make no excuse for returning to again and again. We could have had just one section on the use of the comma splice, but as it tends to keep on creeping back into students' essays even after they have tried to eliminate it, it seems sensible to keep on returning to this pesky, and highly irritating, error.

First, let's go back to Unit 27 and pick up one of the examples there: '*To make any further progress that day was impossible, the rain was far too heavy.' In Unit 28 we offered various ways of rewriting this or repunctuating it because it is, in reality, two sentences joined by a comma: 'To make any further progress that day was impossible' is the first sentence; 'the rain was far too heavy' is the second sentence. But you cannot join or splice sentences by a comma. You can only join sentences by using words such as 'and', 'but', 'or', 'nor', 'so', or by using words such as 'because', 'although'. As we explained in Unit 28, you can make other changes to your sentences and punctuation, but here we want to stress the very simple fact that you cannot join separate sentences by a comma. Nor can you join them by 'however'.

This is a word which if you learn how to use it correctly, by which we actually mean always using the correct punctuation in association with it (and 'however' is a word that nearly always needs supporting punctuation), a great deal of the entire logic of punctuation will suddenly fall into place. Far too often, when people use 'however' they stumble into producing a comma splice. Let's take another sentence from Unit 27 but change it slightly: '*The new approach was first introduced in selected schools in 1987, however, it was in universal use by the middle of the next decade.' This, on the surface, doesn't look like a comma splice simply because there are two commas around 'however'. And it doesn't look like a comma splice because commas do come in pairs around words such as 'however' or little phrases such as 'of course'. And, finally, it doesn't look like a comma splice because it seems to read so well.

But if you read it very carefully you will notice that you pause much longer at the first comma than at the second. You do so because the first comma should be a full stop or semicolon at the end of the sentence. The 'however', then, does not actually join the sentences together as you read, but belongs only to the second sentence. How do you know? The answer is that you can move the word 'however' to another position in the sentence: '*The new approach was first introduced in selected schools in 1987, it was, however, in universal use by the middle of the next decade.' Once you move the 'however' the comma splice becomes plainer, but the other point to grasp here is that we can actually move the word in this way. Contrast this with the way we might use a proper joining word, such as 'but'.

> The new approach was first introduced in selected schools in 1987, but it was in universal use by the middle of the next decade.

This sentence is now grammatically correct, but if we try to move the word 'but' the resulting nonsense becomes clear:

> *The new approach was first introduced in selected schools in 1987, it was in universal use but by the middle of the next decade.

When we say, then, that only words such as 'and', 'but', 'or', 'nor', 'so' can join sentences, what we also mean is that they literally join the sentences and cannot be positioned anywhere else. This is because they are **co-ordinating conjunctions**: they join together or 'co-ordinate' sentences of equal weight. On the other hand words such as 'therefore', 'of course', 'however' are not conjunctions – they are adverbs or simply tags – but can be moved and repositioned in the second sentence:

> The new approach was first introduced in selected schools in 1987; it was in universal use, however, by the middle of the next decade.

Here we have deliberately corrected the punctuation so that there is now a semicolon between the two sentences. That semicolon cannot be replaced by a comma.

The comma splice is a pesk because it eats away at the clear sense of writing. Sentences get joined illegally and then more and more errors creep in as control slips away. But you might have noticed by this stage of the book that nearly all of the errors that overtake a lot of writing concern either the comma or the apostrophe. If you can sort out how to use these two properly, you will be surprised just how easy writing becomes.

▶ **48 The misplaced comma**

What we mean by the 'misplaced comma' is the way in which people insert a comma after the subject of a sentence has been stated. Quite simply, commas have to fall in with the logic of the sentence; they can't just appear willy-nilly after you have been going for a bit. It is, however, easy to understand why misplaced commas creep into sentences. They often appear when a student is attempting to say something fairly complicated in an essay. Consider this example:

> *The otherworldly hell of eternal punishment for the damned, has become a purgatorial hell on earth.

This should be:

> The otherworldly hell of eternal punishment for the damned has become a purgatorial hell on earth.

As always with tackling a problem, it helps if the sentence is broken down into its simplest constituent elements. Here, 'The otherworldly hell of eternal punishment for the damned [subject] has become [verb] a purgatorial hell on earth [complement].' There is no need for a comma after the subject in any simple sentence. It would, of course, be different if a subordinate clause had been introduced: 'The otherworldly hell of eternal punishment for the damned, feared by all men, has become a purgatorial hell on earth.' But there is no subordinate clause in the original version of this sentence.

So why does the student insert a comma? We suspect that because such a large subject has been put forward – a subject that takes nine words to express – it seems appropriate, even if incorrect, to take a momentary pause after it has been stated. This mistake appears again and again in students' essays:

> *The tradition of popular theatre in most of the major towns and cities in nineteenth-century Britain, testifies to the public's need for diversion.

This should be:

> The tradition of popular theatre in most of the major towns and cities in nineteenth-century Britain testifies to the public's need for diversion.

It is fairly clear that the student feels, after such a long opening to the sentence, although it is only stating the subject, that a pause seems to be required. But a pause is not required here. If you are inclined to make this mistake in things you write, you need to make a slight adjustment in terms of how you reflect upon what you have written. You are not paying enough attention to sub-vocalising what you have written, as this would tell you where a pause is required. What you need is to transfer the focus of your attention just a little from the initial conception of your idea to the correct expression of that idea.

▶ 49 You can't invent punctuation; you have to follow the rules rather than make up your own rules

It hardly needs saying that we cannot have everyone making up rules to suit themselves. Imagine if half the population decided that red traffic lights meant 'go' and green meant 'stop'. Of course, sometimes it seems as if that is happening as cars jump the lights or don't move, but we all know what the basic signs mean and what we should do despite these incidents. It's all set out in the Highway Code. Punctuation is no more difficult than the Highway Code, and certainly has fewer signs and rules. The basic signs are:

the exclamation mark
the question mark
the comma
the semicolon
the colon
the dash
the full stop.

The good news is that, in practice, you can get away with using just two or three of these. The bad news is that, far too often, students feel they ought to use all these signs at least once in an essay, and sometimes in a single sentence. Consequently, they drop in the occasional dash, scatter semicolons or cascade commas into perfectly sensible prose, turning it into nonsense. The real problem with punctuation is that if you make up your own rules about how you use it, it shows you up and makes you look foolish. Fortunately, you don't have to make up the rules because the whole business is very simple.

In formal, written English the exclamation mark [!] is rarely used. Indeed, you can go through the whole of life without it, unless, that is, you become a journalist on a tabloid newspaper. You might need the question mark [?] for questions in a letter to your insurance company, although they are likely to know so little about punctuation that you are better off saying to them that 'I have a question to ask about whether my policy covers my computer' if you want an answer. You are, however, unlikely to need the question mark all that often in essays. Occasionally, perhaps, you might want to set up an issue by asking 'What are we to make of this passage?', but there is a lot to be said against the overuse of such devices. And if you are still unsure of how to use the semicolon, the truth is that it is not really a key item of punctuation. As noted previously, the semicolon [;] can replace the full stop where you have two sentences side by side and you wish to indicate that they are dealing with the same issue; you wish, that is, to suggest that there is a link between the two sentences. But the semicolon is another sign that you can stop worrying about. If you don't use it, no one will dock you marks.

The colon [:] is yet another sign that has limited uses and which, most of the time, you can avoid without incurring penalties. Its main function is to introduce a list, or an inset quotation in an essay:

> To be, or not to be, that is the question.

But we could set up this quotation in a different way. We might be writing about the way in which Hamlet ponders the question of death and how he suggests that 'To be or not to be' is the question that troubles us most. We'll come back to the way in which to set out quotations, but the point to notice here is that, in this second example, there is no need to use the colon because the sentence makes perfect sense as it is. The colon is only used where you are indenting and saying to the reader the equivalent of 'Look at this'.

It should be self-evident by now that you cannot avoid using full stops. You would, however, be surprised how many students omit the full stop at the end of a sentence, either because they are rushing or because they did not notice they had reached the end of the sentence. They might well put a capital letter for the start of the next sentence, but forget to put in the basic punctuation mark. The truth is that you cannot avoid full stops, and you cannot avoid commas. These are the key ways in which we control sentences and meanings. They define and shape the boundaries of what we are saying.

▶ 50 An accumulation of irritating errors

This is a student writing an essay about the use of references to theatres in the novels of Charlotte Brontë: '*As a result her translation of the theatre, raises the question of the destiny of women trapped in

The comma

The tricky punctuation mark, without doubt, is the comma. We have listed the six uses of the comma above, but it might be a good idea to reiterate these uses here:

1. *Separating main clauses*

   I like pizza, and every Friday we order a takeaway.

2. *Setting off the introductory element of a sentence*

   Of course, nobody takes Noddy seriously.

3. *Additional clauses at the end of sentences*

   He was sacked from his job, which came as no surprise to anyone.

4. *Subordinate and parenthetical elements in a sentence*

   There are doubts, however, about the authenticity of the painting.

5. *Appositives*

   Victoria Beckham, formerly known as Posh Spice, was among the guests.

6. *Between items in a series or between adjectives that equally modify the same word*

   I checked my shopping list: cakes, jam, bread and butter.

   It was a long, dark tunnel.

This might seem a formidable list, but if you think carefully about it, you will quickly realise that punctuation does come down to the comma. The rest of the signs are simple and have, in the main, one use. The uses of the comma are more diverse, but they are limited and their purpose is always the same – to prevent ambiguity and to clarify meaning. That is true of all punctuation: it is there to serve meaning and preciseness. There is far more involved than just dry and dusty rules. Punctuation is the way you communicate more accurately with your audience.

middle class society without neither an endowment or income.' A corrected version of the sentence might read: 'As a result, her treatment of the theatre raises questions about the destiny of women trapped in middle-class society with neither an endowment nor income.' These are the mistakes in order, mistakes that occur in a great many students' essays:

- The first comma is in the wrong position. The student makes the common mistake of placing a comma after the subject has been stated. The comma needs to appear after the introductory phrase (in this instance, 'As a result'). See Unit 48 on misplaced commas.
- The words 'her translation of the theatre' do not seem to make sense. We suspect that this (see Unit 42) is a case of using the wrong word. She probably means to say 'her treatment of the theatre'. We suspect that the student probably didn't read her work out to herself, so failed to notice that she had written the wrong word.
- The words 'raises the question of' is (see Unit 43) one of those rather awkward, too wordy phrases that could be expressed more succinctly and elegantly. It sounds better as 'raises questions about'.
- The words 'middle class society' should be hyphenated: 'middle-class society.'
- 'without neither' is a form of double negative. It should be either 'with neither' or 'without either'. A moment's thought would reveal whether or not the sentence made sense at this point.

At this point, we wondered whether we had picked up all the errors in this sentence. How did we set about checking? We did what we have kept on urging you to do when you are writing. Check for the basic pattern of a simple sentence:

As a result [introductory phrase], her treatment of the theatre [subject] raises [verb] questions [object] about the destiny of women trapped in middle-class society with neither an endowment nor income [complement].

This does not enable us to check every feature of the sentence, but the fact is that spotting the use of the introductory phrase enables us to get the initial comma correctly positioned. That provides a sound base that we can build upon. If you can get the first comma right, then there is a good chance that everything else will fall into place. But also try to devote a little more time and energy to checking everything you have written. You are always checking in accordance with a small and easy set of rules. But you don't even have to know the rules. Everyone can read over the words they have written. At this point it is not so much knowledge of the rules that matters, but a simple awareness of whether something you have written sounds like English. You might feel less than totally confident about your command of written English, but you are likely to have a formidable in-built awareness of whether something sounds right or sounds wrong.

6 Tricks of the Writer's Trade

▶ **51 Some of the secrets of writing that good writers know**

The last three sections, focusing on the mechanics of how to write correctly, have dealt with things that you might already know. In this section, however, we want to move on to things that you won't perhaps have been taught, to those little hints and wrinkles that can dramatically improve the quality of your writing. These are some of the tricks and skills of the writer's trade, the ruses that writers rely upon to give their work extra impact.

We'll start with a simple point about getting straight into the substance of what you are writing about. A Politics essay might start with the following bold, perhaps provocative, statement: 'The Conservative party has always been at the vanguard of change.' Or an essay could start with the contrary proposition: 'The Labour party has always been deeply conservative.' We have already made the point that it is a good idea to start with a simple, one-statement opening sentence. What is also important, in terms of making your work feel dynamic, is that the subject should appear as early as possible in the sentence. This helps both you and your reader. Your reader can quickly latch on to the essence of what you are writing about. But naming your subject early also gives you a point of reference. The essence of what you are saying is going to get obscured if the sentence is constructed in anything other than the most straightforward manner.

As against the kind of simple sentence patterns we have suggested, many students would opt for something along the following lines: 'A deeply conservative attitude has always been a characteristic of the Labour party.' 'At the vanguard of change we have always found the Conservative party.' These sentences feel back-to-front. They are, as such, unnecessarily complicated. The simple structure of subject/verb/complement is far easier to use and to understand. Why, then, do so many students create an unnecessarily complex structure, obscuring the true subject of their sentences? We suspect that they feel that the convoluted version of the sentences sounds more mature, but it does not strike the reader that way.

The rule about starting with the subject doesn't, however, just apply to opening sentences. It can be sustained as a paragraph continues: 'The Conservative party has always been at the vanguard of change. This is reflected in the leaders they have elected over the years. Benjamin Disraeli, a Jew, dominated the party in the Victorian era, and Margaret Thatcher, a hundred years later, was the first woman prime minister.' These sentences sustain the simple pattern of subject/ verb/complement, keeping the subject close to the verb. It is always a good idea to keep the subject and verb close together; it makes your writing both clear and active. But the main point we want to emphasise here is the advantage to you, as the person steering the sentences along, of announcing your subject early. If you look at books and magazines, you will find that about two-thirds of sentences start with the subject.

The principal reason for departing from this pattern is when a writer starts with an introductory phrase or clause, or some other initial modifying statement. Sometimes this is necessary, or helpful, or provides a welcome degree of variation. After some relatively simple sentences in an essay, you might feel the need for a variation, such as in the use of an adverbial phrase in this sentence: 'In the eyes of many, the emergence of Thatcher was exactly the breath of fresh air a moribund party needed.' But you should generally avoid sentences that start with an excessively long modifying phrase or clause, and also be aware that initial modifying statements can sometimes weaken the impact of what you are writing. It would be a bad idea, for example, to qualify the opening of an essay in this way: 'As many political commentators have observed over the years, the Conservative party has always been at the vanguard of change.' It is usually the case that this kind of initial beating about the bush is superfluous in an essay and can be cut out completely. Generally speaking, the majority of your sentences can and should start by putting the subject first. Many sentences would certainly be improved if they were rewritten putting the subject first.

▶ 52 Think and write in independent clauses

The great difficulty many students experience with writing is that their sentences become tangled as they grapple with trying to say what they want to say. Time and time again we have found ourselves returning essays to students who can tell us what they wanted to say in their essay, but didn't actually manage to say it. As we go through their work, what we draw their attention to is the fact that if they were to simplify the sentences they have written, then their ideas would come across clearly. A common problem is the sentence that starts to make a point, then slips in a dependent clause because it wants to incorporate a related point, and then finds it has to expand again to include another aspect of the point. '*Bill Clinton, during his presidency, which extended for two terms, before which he was governor of Arkansas, just as George W. Bush was governor of Texas, before becoming president of the United States by perhaps the narrowest margin, in fact he lost the popular vote, in modern times.' Obviously, sentences like this stretch and strain. They don't feel comfortable and they don't offer an impression of being in charge. If you try to track the logic of this faulty sentence, you will see that it starts to say something about Bill Clinton (who is actually the subject of the sentence), but then gets waylaid and never gets round to saying anything about him. In the end it simply falls apart.

The answer to this kind of traffic snarl-up is to opt for more sentences that make a point in a single clause without any kind of interruption. Of course, too many single-clause sentences would become tedious, but we aren't saying use only single-clause sentences. What we are saying is that you should make your point cleanly and clearly; then, if you want, add one or more independent clauses (that is to say, units more or less capable of standing alone as separate sentences) to the sentence. But don't incorporate or add on too many distractions. Save these for the next sentence and subsequent sentences. Our Clinton/Bush sentence was far too busy. Cut out the asides, deviations and qualifications, most of which are likely to prove irrelevant anyway, and focus on making the point in an independent clause, and then seamlessly make the transition to the next sentence and the next sentence: 'Bill Clinton served two terms as president of the United States. Before this he was governor of Arkansas, just as George W. Bush was governor of Texas before becoming president. Bush, who actually lost the popular vote, was elected by perhaps the narrowest margin in modern times.' The disentangling of the original has depended upon creating separate sentences for each step forward, and clear-cut subordinate clauses in the second and third sentences linked to the main subject.

In further refining what has been written, the confident writer would then try to lose a few words along the way. 'Bill Clinton served two terms as president of the United States. Before this he was governor of Arkansas, just as George W. Bush was governor of Texas before becoming president. Bush was elected by the narrowest margin in modern times.' A degree of detail might have been sacrificed, but this is more than compensated for by the gain in clarity. In fact, you won't be going far wrong if more than half of your sentences consist of one or more unadorned and uninterrupted independent clauses. If a sentence has to become more busy and complicated – and some sentences have to – try to limit yourself to three dependent clauses. The essence of the issue, therefore, is the importance of a plain and unencumbered style. You might not get the expression of your idea right first time, but the meaning can be clarified by cutting. The point to grasp is that what you are trying to say can be said best if you just get on and say it, without too many unnecessary asides.

▶ 53 The rule of proximity

What have we said so far? Make it clear what your subject is, and as your essay continues make sure that the reader is always kept in touch with your subject. This means avoiding too many asides or messy distractions in sentences; essentially, you want a series of independent clauses that stick with the subject. Each sentence, or step of a sentence, picks up from the point where things have arrived, and pursues the subject further. Think in terms of manageable idea capsules. A writer lacking confidence tries to link all the idea capsules together. A confident writer, by contrast, will often devote a separate sentence to each idea capsule.

The reader of your work should never be put in the position of having to search for the sense of what you are saying. What you have written should be you serving up, in the clearest possible way, the meaning of what you are saying. What helps in this is not just writing in sentences of manageable length, but also bearing in mind a technique called the 'rule of proximity'. What this means is that those parts of a sentence that connect with each other to establish order must be positioned as near as possible to each other. There is clearly something wrong with this sentence: '*Fast bikes are an obsession of many men, some with speeds exceeding two hundred miles an hour.' It is presumably the bikes rather than the men that are fast. But this sentence gets in a muddle. How can it be sorted out? Find your simple sentence: 'Fast bikes are an obsession of many men.' The additional information can then become an additional sentence. 'Some of these bikes have speeds exceeding two hundred miles an hour.' Or it can be slipped in as a subordinate clause alongside the subject: 'Fast bikes, some with speeds exceeding two hundred miles an hour, are an obsession of many men.' This might seem a trivial point to emphasise, but it is a failing in writing that reflects the much wider problem of failing to write in simple sense units.

The mistake made above was one of trying to include extra information about the bikes too late in the sentence. The result is a common error in which the new information ended up modifying 'men' instead of bikes. The trick is always to make sure that you keep information together. If you look at the original sentence, you will see that the word 'men' is followed by the word 'some'. The word 'some' here must refer to the men because that is the last noun mentioned. In terms of grammar, the phrase 'some with speeds exceeding two hundred miles an hour' here describes the men, not the bikes. Of course, most people will realise what is meant by the sentence, but that does not make it correct.

▶ 54 Perform what you have written

We hesitated before including this point. We feared we might be thought of as eccentric in that we not only read out what we have written but also deliver it as a kind of dramatic performance to an imaginary audience. It seemed a good idea to check whether other people had the same peculiar habit. To our surprise, a lot of other writers told us that they, too, relied upon this strategy. It obviously isn't possible to do this in an examination (although it is a good idea to sub-vocalise what you have written as you go along), but with an essay it can help you judge whether the essay is working if you do some of the following things:

- Read the essay out loud, to an imaginary audience, in a rather theatrical way, making exaggerated pauses where commas appear and at the end of each sentence.
- Take normal amounts of breath; if you run out of breath during a sentence, then clearly something is going wrong.
- Is it possible to deliver what you have written as a speech? If not, then the chances are that the sentences are too intricate and convoluted.

Some people who use this technique tell us that they accompany their performance with hand movements, signalling commas and signalling subordinate clauses. It might sound absurd, but what they are doing with their hand movements is almost modelling the sentences in front of them. The result of this approach tends to be a move towards simpler and shorter sentences, but sentences which, because they can be delivered as a dramatic performance, always make a striking impact on the reader.

▶ 55 Don't waste words

This is the start of an essay by a Chemistry student. For their first essay at university the members of the class were asked to write about 'The Scientific Method': 'The hallmark of science is defined as the method of basing general statements on accumulated observations of specific instances.' There is a good sentence here struggling to get out. The problem is that the student uses too many words. The sentence can be cut back to 'Science bases general statements on the accumulated observations of specific instances.' What we have done here is make the subject of the sentence as clear as possible by cutting back the number of words. We might have lost a nuance of meaning, but the gain in clarity means that we have actually gained, rather than lost, meaning.

Time and time again you must consider whether a sentence is too wordy: 'I will speak to you individually about this later.' Does 'individually' serve any real purpose? Wouldn't the sentence carry more impact, and mean more or less what it already says, if it was cut? 'I will speak to you about this later.' The start of a sentence is a place where superfluous words can often accumulate to little effect: 'It should be appreciated that Charles Dickens was not actually a Londoner by birth.' Why not just inform us that: 'Charles Dickens was not a Londoner by birth.' The start of the sentence has been cut, plus 'actually', which more often than not serves little purpose in writing or, for that matter, speech. It is a redundant reinforcer, intended, in a way that never quite works, to lend more weight to a sentence. A lot of radio and television presenters seem to use 'actually' in just about every sentence. If you hear the word, try to decide whether it is serving any real purpose in what is said. In every sentence that you write, remind yourself that you need to 'write tight'.

▶ 56 Use the most direct words

A short word is always to be preferred to a long word. Short words are, quite simply, stronger than long ones. Think, for example, of a classic pop song by the Supremes: 'Stop in the name of love.' It is a wonderful opening line that immediately gets attention. 'Desist in the name of love' sounds and is absurd, partly because the verb 'desist' usually requires an object: 'Desist stroking your beard that way.' But 'desist' is also officialese and pretentious. The point about short words is that they are plain in their sense and tell the reader or listener what they want to hear. For this reason they possess an elegance born out of clarity.

This may seem 'erroneous' to some, especially people who prefer erroneous to the simple word 'wrong'. But why would anyone choose 'erroneous' over 'wrong'? Is it because they think some of their listeners might not understand 'erroneous', whereas everybody understands 'wrong'? This is something to be aware of when you are reading around a subject. Some writers and speakers deliberately choose words on the basis that they are not commonly used. Or they try to pick out words that will sound grand or impressive. They will, for example, 'furnish you with proof', rather than 'provide' or 'give' it. Government ministers will always talk about 'reductions', not 'cuts', because they wish to get away from the reality of what they are doing.

The other reason for using direct words is that they enable you to control what you are saying. Most student essays that fall apart do so, in part, because the sentences fail to make sense, but also because they use the wrong words. Striving to impress, or perhaps anxious to do well, students pluck words out of the air or make them up rather than stick to plain, forceful words that they know and feel at ease with. Thus things are said to 'commence' rather than 'begin'; battles 'terminate' instead of 'ending'. In each case the student is thinking about how to impress rather than how to inform. If you find yourself doing this, then the only real solution is to go through your essay and make sure that each word is actually contributing to the sense and argument of the essay. If it sounds like pretentious waffle – 'the ideology of the text interpellates the reader in a deconstructive framework of post-modern contradiction' – then it probably is so.

This is not to say that you have to write in a baby style, never using grown-up words. Direct words are the words that are most appropriate and most useful to you as you write or speak. But sometimes there is only a long word available to do the job. If you do wish to talk about the 'ideology' of a text, then that is the word to use; it is the most direct word. In the example in the previous paragraph, however, it gets entangled in a whole cluster of other words and concepts rather than being used on its own in a relevant way. There is, then, a middle style of writing. Use direct words and use short words whenever you can, but don't avoid long words if they are the right word for the job.

▶ 57 Short words to end a sentence

You should always be aiming for simplicity and directness in expression. If you perform what you have written, something you might notice is that in most sentences the chief stress comes at the end. The reason for this is very simple. It is only as we reach the end of a sentence that the meaning of the sentence is finally revealed or delivered. It makes sense, therefore, to aim for a very clear degree of impact at the end of a sentence, which is helped by concluding with the point you really want to get across – and with that point stated as simply as possible. Many years ago, a British prime minister, Harold Macmillan, famously told the nation, 'You've never had it so good.' Why this works is because it is so direct and to the point. Nobody would remember the phrase if he had said: 'You've never enjoyed such personal affluence.' Or: 'You've never experienced such good fortune.' Wherever possible, therefore, try to end a sentence with an emphatic and simple word.

In the same area, always avoid trailing off into additional clauses. This is again a recurrent failing in students' essays. Having made the point, they then want to add a bit more, just to be on the safe side. But the rule is, make your point, and then move on to the next sentence. It would undermine the impact of what Macmillan said if it became 'You've never had it so good, thanks to my government.' Allowing the sentence to trail away like this lessens its force. In writing essays, what you need to resist is the impulse to add another bit to the sentence just to make the meaning clearer or to elaborate the point. Nine times out of ten it will not have this effect. Indeed, you might find that you are starting to produce a series of comma-spliced sentences, as you add a bit and add a bit. That last sentence would be a better sentence if we followed our own advice. It can be rewritten as 'Indeed, as you add a bit and add a bit, you might find that you are starting to produce a series of comma-spliced sentences.' If Macmillan had wanted to claim responsibility for the good fortune of the country, it would be best expressed as 'Thanks to my government, you've never had it so good.'

An opening phrase always has a great deal to be said for it in preference to an extra clause at the end.

As a student, you might look at one of your essays and realise that it is full of sentences that just trail on and on. For corrective surgery, you can do one of three things.

- You can break off and start a new sentence
- You can see if the closing clause can be relocated as an opening phrase or at some other point in the sentence.
- You can, surprisingly often, just cut the extra bit that grows on the end of the sentence, on the basis that it adds little if nothing.

All of this is particularly relevant in the opening paragraph of an essay, where the writer does not know how much to tell the reader about the essay that is going to follow. 'Dickens, as we will see, writes from the heart of the Victorian city, expressing its fears but also its aspirations, in novels that get lost in the labyrinthine streets of London.' It would be enough to finish the paragraph with 'Dickens, as we will see, writes from the heart of the Victorian city.' But if we wanted to include all of the idea, it might be best to position the subsidiary point in a new sentence: 'Dickens, as we will see, writes from the heart of the Victorian city. In novels that get lost in labyrinthine streets, he expresses its fears but also its aspirations.' As you can see, we have split the initial cumbersome sentence into two, and then repositioned the closing words as an opening clause in the second sentence. It is this kind of simple act of juggling and tidying that transforms writing. Attention to the idea is complemented by attention to how the idea can be made to arrest the reader's attention.

▶ 58 Active writing

Much of what we have just said connects with the need for writing actively. Time after time, aspiring writers will be told to keep their work active and avoid the passive, but what does this mean? Usually, the advice will be scribbled in a margin note saying, 'Use the active voice', or, 'Avoid the passive voice'. What is meant by this is how verbs can be used. Most verbs can be used in either an active or a passive form. The difference is easy to grasp. In the following sentence the verb is in the **active voice**:

> The dog bit the man.

An active verb is one where the subject – here, the dog – performs the action of the verb. The passive voice is the other way round:

> The man was bitten by the dog.

Here the subject – the man – is not doing the action but is on the receiving end of it. The action is done to the man by the dog.

You might wonder why anyone would bother about such seemingly petty details. Does it really matter which way round we put the information since it all amounts to the same thing? In both cases it is clear that it is the dog that bit the man, not the man who bit the dog. If you stop to think about it, however, you will soon see that most of the time in our daily lives we use the active voice:

> I hate washing-up

> The police caught the man quickly

> We will write to you next week

We use the active voice because it conveys information quickly and directly. It tells the reader what is going on in the sentence. There is something slightly clumsy and indirect about passive sentences; they tend to leave the reader with the job of working out quite what is meant:

> It has been recommended by doctors that more fruit should be eaten daily.

This sounds formal and weighty, but how much clearer it becomes in the active voice:

> Doctors recommend that we eat more fruit daily.

There is just a hint of doubt in the passive form of this sentence, as if doctors had not directly recommended the eating of fruit.

Like many concepts in grammar and writing, the terms 'active' and 'passive' can seem complicated the first time you meet them, and even easy to confuse. You can, however, easily recognise the passive voice by the way it is formulated: it has two parts to the verb, 'was bitten'. A useful test is to remember that the passive is nearly always made up of parts of the verb 'to be' (here, 'was') plus a past participle (here, 'bitten'). A second test is that in passive sentences the doer of the action always comes after the verb.

> The man was arrested by police.

> Trees were damaged by storms.

Most people who write about style recommend that you avoid the passive as much as you possibly can. This is good advice, especially if you find you are writing long, elaborate sentences that take ages to say what is going on and don't make any real point. Usually they can be rewritten in the active voice, often with some words lost. But, as with this last sentence, passive sentences can be slipped in without any serious damage. We could have written 'Usually you can rewrite such sentences in the active voice, often losing some words.' And that is a rather better, because simpler and, therefore, more effective, sentence. The real point is, however, that the more you know what you are doing with a sentence, the more you can control your reader and your argument.

► **59 Judging tone**

What one writes has to be mechanically correct, and also sound and feel like English. But there is an additional factor involved in writing, which is finding the right tone. It applies everywhere. If you missed a class, you shouldn't send a note saying, 'Hey, a million apologies. You know how it is! Like, I overslept, again. What am I like?' A note of apology written in such a casual tone might provoke the response: 'What you are like is someone who is going to get a low mark.' But how do you know if what you are writing sounds slangy or too collo-quial? It might be that there are people out there who think it would be entirely appropriate to describe a character in a novel or a character in history as 'well hard'. The fact is, however, that most students can tell the difference between formal and informal modes of expression, and if they cannot, there is a good chance that the incongruity of certain words and phrases should strike them if they read their work out loud to themselves.

While one problem is a slangy, colloquial style, another is that of essays that sound far too pretentious. Don't strain for effect. Consider a sentence like this: 'The text embraces an apotheosis of manhood that finds its symbolic centre in the representation of certain gendered characteristics.' It does not really convey very much to the reader. But if it becomes a bit less ambitious in terms of vocabulary, it works a lot better: 'The play focuses on a number of male figures who represent an ideal of manhood.' What is wrong with the original sentence is that it is trying too hard to impress and so goes over the top, crowding big words into the sentence. And having done it once, the student will be forced to go on, inflating every sentence in the same way. It is much more stylish, however, to use big words mixed in with simple, clear vocabulary. That way your points become much more telling, and much more persuasive. Remember, your reader will be just as interested in how you write as in what you have to say.

We have mentioned the idea of style here deliberately. Style is no more than the right words in the right order. As you develop your writing, you will become more and more conscious of your vocabulary and how to vary the order of your sentences. Brief sentences can make a point. Longer sentences, perhaps carefully nuanced to include small details or to recognise another perspective, can give the reader pleasure. But not if they straggle on endlessly, saying nothing and simply filling out the lines. Noticing how you shape your sentences will help transform writing from a chore into a craft that can be rewarding in more than one sense. We live in a world where communicating well, and being able to write sensibly for your audience, is a valuable skill; if you can write well, you start your career with a tremendous advantage.

▶ 60 Use the conventions of writing to organise your thoughts

When someone writes in a way that is awkward, confusing or just plain bad, something odd has happened. They have something they want to say, but the act of writing lets them down. It can be compared to trying to juggle if you don't know how to juggle; all of us know that frantic feeling as things fall all over the place. Understandably, a lot of people dread writing for precisely this kind of reason. But there is only a very small distance between the person who dreads writing and the person who is a confident writer.

The confident writer is someone who knows just how straightforward good writing is. They are aware of some simple principles:

Write in simple, independent sentences.
Start with the subject.
Keep subject and verb together.
Read your work out loud.
Use direct words.
Write in the active voice.
Use a sensible tone and vocabulary.

What the confident writer has also grasped is that writing, rather than being something that defies control, involves a simple set of rules that help you to say exactly what you want to say. In the same way, if you have learnt how to drive you are equipped to drive fast along motorways. You are not doing anything different from what you would be doing on a quiet country road: steering, changing gear, stopping when necessary and remaining alert. The basic techniques of driving steer you through any situation. In the same way, it is the simple rules of writing that enable you to say what you want to say.

It might surprise you to hear that people who have written a great many books become more and more conscious of, and pay more and more attention to, the basic rules of writing. They know that the more ambitious their work becomes the more vital it is to check what they have written against the simple ground rules. These fundamental rules are:

- knowing the pattern of simple, compound and complex sentences;
- knowing how to make use of the six (main) rules relating to the use of commas in order to add a phrase or clause at the start or end or in the middle of a sentence;
- recognising when a comma splice has been used, and knowing how to remedy the fault;
- recognising when a fragment has been used, and knowing how to remedy the fault;
- reading the sentence out loud to check that the words say what the writer wants them to say.

These (if we count the point about commas as six points) are the ten things that you need to be aware of in order to write correct and coherent sentences. It really is as simple as this. Of course, where many students find that their real problems start is when they begin to combine sentences to write an essay. That is the issue that we turn to in the next section. But for the moment we want to draw together this first part of the book by summarising the ten things you need to know that will enable you to produce correct and convincing sentences.

Sentences: the ten things you need to know and need to be able to do:

1. Know the basic pattern of all sentences – the structure of subject/verb/complement (or object).

2–7. Know how to employ the six main rules relating to the use of commas:

    (i)   in order to add a phrase or clause at the start of a sentence;

    (ii) punctuating linked main clauses;

    (iii) before a phrase at the end of a sentence;

    (iv) adding subordinate elements into a sentence;

    (v) adding words in apposition;

    (vi) separating items in a list.

8. Recognise when a comma splice has been used, and know how to remedy the fault.

9. Recognise when a fragment has been used, and know how to remedy the fault.

10. Read each sentence out loud to check that the words say what you want them to say, and that they say this in a way that you believe to be both mechanically correct and aesthetically pleasing.

7 Essay Writing: Structure

▶ 61 First principles of essay writing

Everyone finds essay writing difficult. No matter how much research, planning and preparation you have done, there comes that awful moment when you sit down with a blank piece of paper or a blank screen and cannot think what to say. Eventually, of course, the words do come, and, after much sweat and tears, you have a completed essay. At this stage, most people are very unsure whether what they have written is any good or not. They hand their work in and nervously hope for the best.

It should not be like this. Essay writing should not resemble wandering into a maze with a vague hope that you will eventually emerge safely on the other side. The reason why it is so often like this is because most people do not have a method they can call upon in writing an essay. The majority of students will have done a great deal of work on preparing their material and points, but will have little idea how to present and discuss what they have discovered. And some of the teaching they receive, particularly at university, may not offer much direct assistance. The lectures will have pointed the student in the right direction for the content of an essay, but it is very unlikely that the lecturer will have offered much advice about how to turn raw content into an effective essay. Indeed, there often seems to be an assumption that nature will take its course: that the cleverer students will, perhaps instinctively, know how to make the best use of what they have been taught. It need not be like this. Education is about acquiring knowledge and skills; the system has failed if it just provides you with knowledge while assuming that it can do nothing about teaching you the necessary skills.

Fortunately, the skills involved in essay writing are easy to grasp and easy to put into practice. It is these skills, which it seems reasonable to call 'the secrets of effective essay writing', that we consider in this and the next two sections. These secrets will not solve all the problems associated with essay writing, but they should deal with most of the difficulties that you are likely to encounter along the way. They are also secrets that can be called upon for any essay in any subject; whatever the subject, the principles of effective essay writing remain the same. We can start with the fact that there are two fundamentally different ways of tackling an essay. The high-risk strategy is to start with a vague hope that your essay will find a shape, focus and direction as you go along. The result, almost always, is an essay that rambles, and in which the reader has to more or less dig out and piece together what is being argued. Paragraphs tend to go on until they start to look too long, at which point the student starts a fresh paragraph. This way of writing an essay, where the case evolves organically, can work well, but it can also lead to confusion and chaos.

The alternative approach is to start with a very clear idea of the shape and structure of the essay, and then to develop your ideas within this predetermined form. In fact, we will be suggesting that it is a good idea to know in advance exactly how many paragraphs you are going to have in an essay, how long each paragraph is going to be, and the function of each paragraph. Some teachers and lecturers have reservations about this approach; they feel that it stifles the imagination and creative thinking. But the fact is that a predetermined structure to an essay actually liberates the imagination: the student can concentrate on content because the form of the essay is looking after itself.

▶ 62 The shape of an essay

What is this miraculous essay structure that can, seemingly, solve all your problems? Many of the pieces of work that you will be asked to produce at school, college or university will have a word limit somewhere between 500 and 3000 words. It is a format for this average essay that we intend to describe here (we present a strategy for longer essays of, say, 2500–3000 words, and for report writing, in Section 9). The best place to start is with a fairly firm idea of how many paragraphs your essay will contain. We suggest that eight paragraphs is the most suitable number for most essays, that is, an introduction and conclusion and six main paragraphs. At this point, even before considering the subject matter of your essay, you can establish some idea about what is going to happen in each of these paragraphs.

Paragraph 1 simply introduces the topic. Unless there is some very good reason for it not being so, this should always be a short paragraph. About ten to twelve lines should be sufficient. There is no point in introducing unnecessary complications at the beginning of an essay.

This is where many people go wrong. Right at the start, they introduce more material and more ideas than they can handle. Just as an essay should open with a short paragraph, it makes sense to conclude with a short final paragraph of about ten to twelve lines. At the end you are simply pulling the threads together; the last paragraph is not the place for embarking upon a new line of argument.

In between the introduction and the conclusion, you have the body of the essay: six paragraphs where an amazing amount of ground can be covered, and a great many intelligent, even brilliant, things can be said. It is a good idea to aim at making each of these paragraphs more or less the same length (about half to two-thirds of a side). Think of these paragraphs as well-ordered chunks of information and ideas that you are feeding to your reader. If a paragraph is too short, the point you were trying to make will only have been half-developed. If a paragraph is too long, it is outstaying its welcome; the main point will have been drowned in a sea of words.

The paragraphs each have a role:

- 2 and 3 – start to explore the issue;
- 4 and 5 – push the issue along;
- 6 and 7 – the essay arrives somewhere.

If you reflect on this pattern, what might strike you is that in constructing an argument you are, in a sense, constructing a story with a beginning, a middle and an end. The first third of the essay introduces and starts to establish a theme, the middle section complicates the issue, and then, as in every good story, there should be something just a little unsuspected about where the narrative arrives in the final third. We summarise the overall structure of an essay to our students in this way:

-             Introduction
- 2 and 3 Set it up
- 4 and 5 Push it along
- 6 and 7 Push your luck
- 8   Conclusion

The phrase 'push your luck' might surprise you. What we mean by this is that in order to distinguish yourself in an essay you have to move beyond received ideas or move into more complex territory at some point in an essay; the appropriate place to do this is in the final third of what you are writing.

One of the advantages of a structure like this is that it helps you pace an essay. You are in control of an argument that is unfolding and developing in a steady and controlled way. Over and over again, we have read essays where students tie themselves up in knots almost from the outset; the sentences become convoluted as the students endeavour to juggle with too much material. But a predetermined plan means that complications can develop naturally, and in a controlled way, as the essay advances. Something that can help in achieving this kind of clarity is to write with a certain audience, preferably one person, in mind. Your imagined audience should not be a teacher or a lecturer, but your mum or dad, or grandparent, or younger brother or sister. You need to be taking them along with you at every stage of the essay; each paragraph should be providing them with as much, and no more, in the way of ideas and information as they can handle, and no more. Another way of putting this is to say that an essay should not be bombarding the reader with an attempt to appear stunningly clever from the outset. A sensible student keeps things relatively simple at the beginning, with complications in the argument developing in each of the paragraph steps. (We should add at this point that the same three-part logic of 'set it up/push it along/push your luck' can be applied to an essay of any length, not just to eight-paragraph essays. We deal with writing longer essays in Section 9.)

▶ 63 Working with a paragraph plan: theory into practice

You might be very sceptical about whether the general-purpose essay plan we have described will work in the subject you are studying. Indeed, it might be that you have an essay question in front of you now, and can see no possibility of constructing an answer along the lines we have suggested. This is the point, therefore, at which we need to provide some examples. What links all these illustrations is the fact that a certain kind of logic – the logic of the shape of an argument – runs through every piece of written work. You might be writing about pollution, how to turn round a failing business, mental health legislation, developments in biotechnology, or Napoleon Bonaparte, but the actual shape and logic of an argument will be very much the same regardless of the subject.

You have to start by introducing the basic principles and substance of the issue under consideration; the reader of your essay needs basic information, definitions of essential terms and points of reference. But you cannot continue for too long with laying the foundations. For one thing, your reader's interest will begin to wane. After a couple of paragraphs, therefore, you need to develop some of the implications of the material and ideas you have established in the first third of the essay. And it would be possible to just continue at this level, discussing an implication, going on to another implication and so on, but it is again the case that your reader's attention will begin to drift if the discussion begins to lose energy and onward drive. In order to maintain interest, you have to find a fresh level of complication in what you are writing about.

But more is involved than just holding the reader's interest. It is the logic of argument that is at issue here, whereby propositions are first of all considered, their implications are then followed up, and, if the discussion has been working as it should, the essay should arrive somewhere, perhaps somewhere that you might not have expected to arrive. The moment you realise that this sequence of development underlies an essay, it makes writing any individual essay a lot easier. You are not wandering into a maze, but treading a well-worn path. This does not mean that you will be saying the same things as everyone else; on the contrary, just as, for example, the established form of the sonnet permits an endless variety of poems, a simple essay plan permits an infinite variety of distinctive essays.

Let us look a little more closely at how an essay question might be tackled. In a General Studies course, you might be asked to discuss the following proposition: 'The best way of cutting crime is to send more offenders to prison.' A Law or Sociology or Social Policy student might have specialised knowledge that they could call upon, but in a General Studies paper this kind of question is testing two things: your general knowledge, and your ability to construct an argument. In your introductory paragraph, you might say that opinions are divided, that some people favour a stiffer sentencing policy whereas others dispute the effectiveness of prison as a deterrent. You could then devote paragraphs 2 and 3 to outlining reasons why sending more people to prison would be a good idea, but then, having dealt with this stance, it is time to move on. Paragraphs 4 and 5, therefore, could present the case against sending more people to prison. You then reach a point, about two-thirds of the way through the essay, where a great deal of the obvious ground has been covered and a great many of the obvious things have been said. It now becomes necessary to consider how the argument can be pushed further in the last third of the essay. There is no right or wrong answer available here; it is up to you how you push the argument along. You could, for example, decide to focus on the example of the United States, with a very high prison population, but also a very high crime rate. This might prompt you to conclude that prison, by its effect on criminals, leads to further crime, rather than crime leading to prison. The important thing is to find a fresh direction, but one that builds upon what you have established in the earlier sections of the essay.

What if you had been asked to write about Napoleon and his defeat by the British at the Battle of Waterloo? You might have been asked whether his defeat was inevitable. In your introductory paragraph, you could familiarise your reader with Napoleon and his final campaign, and pose the question about why he was defeated. Paragraphs 2 and 3 might give reasons (for example, the strength of the nations ranged against him) that guaranteed his defeat. Paragraphs 4 and 5 could then become 'on the other hand' paragraphs, suggesting reasons (for example, his tactical brilliance as a military commander) why his defeat was surprising. Paragraphs 6 and 7 would then need to extend the issue. You might decide to argue that the arguments on both sides are so substantial that really it was only a matter of luck that the result went one way rather than another. Or you could decide to broaden your frame of reference, producing a possibly more sophisticated argument in which you argued that all revolutionaries throughout history who have challenged the established order of nations, in the way that Napoleon did, have eventually come to grief.

What about an essay question that asked you to consider the problem of turning round a failing business? Paragraph 1 might suggest that while businesses do fail, there is often a strategy that could revive their fortunes. Paragraphs 2 and 3 could focus on the initial problem of determining why a certain business was performing badly (it could be a problem with the product, poor management, poor marketing and distribution, or any manner of reasons). Paragraphs 4 and 5 could then move on to possible remedies. In paragraphs 6 and 7, you could go into more detail about a remedy for the specific example your essay might have been dealing with, or, if you had been talking in general terms up until this point, you could now turn to a specific example. The final paragraph, paragraph 8, will not have all that much to add, but it should be able to wrap up the issue, rather implying that the way to tackle a business problem is not unlike the methodical step-by-step approach you have deployed in your essay. Can you see how the logic of how to construct an argument is always very straightforward? In a sense, you start at the beginning, look at how the issue develops, and then, very distinctly, in the last third of the essay, see where all of this gets you.

▶ 64 Look at this essay: consider its underlying logic, structure and pace

Look at this essay by an English Literature student. It does not matter if you are not studying English, as what we are concerned with here is the form of the essay, the way, that is, in which, in a deceptively simple manner, it efficiently assembles a very interesting case. The student is writing about Thomas Hardy's novel *Far from the Madding Crowd*.

Writing in *Far from the Madding Crowd*

Writing plays a central role in *Far from the Madding Crowd*. At one level, it is used fairly straightforwardly for conveying messages. In addition, however, it is a medium which invests the writer with authority; it offers stability, and characters often try to conceal themselves behind it. In hiding in writing, though, the characters emphasise their secretive natures. Writing then hinders, rather than promotes, communication. We begin to see that in the changing world of Hardy's novel the written word is being undermined: it no longer reflects an unquestionable black and white authority, but signals that the stability of the old order seems to be disintegrating.

The written word never just delivers a plain and simple message. Farmer James Everdene has his name painted on the side of his carriage, the expense of the lettering highlighting his status in the community. Joseph Poorgrass, however, 'could never mind which way to turn the J's and E's . . .',[1] and this makes Everdene 'cuss, and call thee a fool . . . when 'a seed his name looking so inside-out-like' (p. 159). While it is prestigious to have your name painted, to have it written incorrectly merely serves to make it into a mockery. What is also conveyed here is the connection between the written form and social class. We see this again when Bathsheba first appears at the farm, gathers her workers together and writes in front of them: 'She sat down at a table and opened the time-book, pen in her hand, with a canvas money-bag beside her' (p. 127). Sitting at a table with pen in hand, Bathsheba creates an impression of authority and organisation. No writing has yet taken place, but a message is conveyed: this woman is educated and in control. Indeed, it would seem that writing acts as the medium of authority and control, yet, as is evident in Poorgrass's errors, if writing is not strictly regulated then it can undermine the very authority that it is intended to enhance.

While writing can be functional, it is also used as a source of comfort. Oak dreams of putting his and Bathsheba's marriage announcement in the newspaper: '"And when the wedding was over, we'd have it put in the newspaper list of marriages."' Bathsheba delights in this idea: '"Dearly I should like that"' (p. 79). A name in print is a privilege; it would be something solid to hang on to, as well as a public declaration that carries almost as much weight as the marriage itself. Boldwood also clings on to the written word as he labels 'an extraordinary collection of articles . . . carefully wrapped in paper . . . "Bathsheba Boldwood"' (p. 446). By attaching Bathsheba to his own name in writing, Boldwood deludes himself into believing that she will marry him; he needs the stability of the written form, as her spoken agreement is not sufficient. While the characters often see the written form as a concrete truth, however, they also begin to hide behind it, and even, as in Boldwood's case, manipulate it to their own advantage. By these actions the medium of writing begins to lose its validity; it is used for comfort as well as communication.

This is evident again and again in the novel: writing is the medium which can be resorted to when all else has failed. We see it when Bathsheba turns down Boldwood's proposal:

> She now sank down into a chair, wild and perturbed by all these new and fevering sequences. Then she jumped up with a manner of decision, and fetched her desk from a side table.   (p. 251)

The thought of writing a letter transforms Bathsheba's mood from being perturbed to being decisive. A letter, like the desk that it is written on, is stable; it is a solid concept to hold on to while emotions run 'wild'. Bathsheba also relies on written words when she conceals herself in the attic after the scandal concerning Troy and Fanny has broken: '"Bring up some books – not new ones. I haven't heart to read anything new. . . . Bring me *Love in a Village* . . . "' (p. 367). The old and familiar romance provides a certain stability in this disturbed part of her life. But the written word here does not aid the communication which is needed between Bathsheba and the outside world; paradoxically, it keeps her indoors, passing time but sheltered from harsh reality.

The use of writing or reading merely as a pastime can lead to its misuse; this is most obvious in the Valentine that Bathsheba sends to Boldwood: 'Bathsheba, a small yawn upon her mouth, took the pen, and with off-hand serenity directed the missive to Boldwood' (p. 147). The implications of this 'trifling trick' (p. 259) emphasise the power of the written word, as Boldwood is convinced that '"the letter must have had an origin and a motive"' (p. 149). The card causes Boldwood's imagination to run wild as he lusts after whoever sent it: 'some *woman*'s hand had travelled softly over the paper. . . . Her mouth – were the lips red or pale, plump or creased?' (p. 150). Boldwood, indeed, never questions the sincerity of the card; it is written and, therefore, is beyond question. He then proceeds to build fantasies upon it. At this point reading and writing become a matter of expressing sexuality. Valentine's day was one of the few days on which women were permitted by society to express their sexual feelings. On the one hand, therefore, the act of sending a Valentine's card is an expression of liberation. But the unreliability of a written document complicates the issue. The Valentine does not provide a direct access to true feelings. Moreover, the fact that sexuality is channelled by writing ensures that it is controlled by a polite, yet deceptive, social form. By sending a fake Valentine, Bathsheba makes a mockery of Valentine's day, emphasising that writing is not always trustworthy, but the potential for confusion exists in the very activity of writing.

It might seem logical to assume, however, that, while cards and letters may not be trustworthy, a printed text, for example a newspaper, must be reliable. Even this assumption is undermined, however, for when Troy vanishes, although Bathsheba feels that he is still alive, 'two circumstances conjoined to shake [this view]. The first was a short paragraph in the local newspaper' (p. 388). The printed text here has the power to make Bathsheba question her heart-felt feeling. There is a sense that if some-thing is important enough to be printed in the newspaper then it must be true. The newspaper report of Troy's death is a crucial exception to the rule, however, and the error helps bring about serious consequences, as it boosts Boldwood's hopes of marrying Bathsheba. What is read in the newspapers is believed, for the community sees a printed text as being as important as something written in stone. A tombstone is, of course, the most emphatic form of writing. To have something as final as death inscribed in stone for all to see gives the written word an awe-inspiring authority. However, Troy's gravestone is a fake, for it is erected before his death, and thus undermines the validity of words, even those written in stone. Similarly, although the words on Fanny's coffin were only 'scrawled' (p. 351) in chalk, the fact that Oak rubbed away '*and child*' (p. 351), in order to lessen Bathsheba's pain, shows how even words on a coffin can be deceptive; they are easily rubbed away in order to produce a different meaning. Whether chalked, printed or inscribed in stone, the written form is always open to question, and when writing is questioned the founda-tions of what society believes in are shaken.

Society depends upon what it has inherited, and the authority of the written word is one aspect of this. Troy, however, is an exception to most of society's rules. It is interesting that while many characters conceal themselves in writing, manipulate it or use it as an alternative to meeting people, Troy is exempt from such behaviour. Pennyways is aware of Troy's awkward situation and believes, like other characters, that communication by letter would be the correct way of dealing with a complicated and emotional problem: '"Why not write to her? 'Tis a very queer corner that you have got into"' (p. 426). Troy's response to this is to 'empty his glass in one draught' and declare that he 'shall be there . . . before nine' (p. 428). Troy always acts quickly and on impulse. Understandably, Bathsheba, who writes to both Boldwood and Oak, sees little point in writing to Troy: 'A letter to keep him away could not reach him in time, even if he should be disposed to listen to it' (p. 272). Writing is seen as a form of control, for it is a socially acceptable way to communicate. Troy, not accepting this convention, must be viewed with suspicion. He shatters the stability of Weatherbury by forcing the community to question their old traditions; he is the representative of a new untrustworthy world.

The validity of the written form is an old belief that the characters cling on to, for they hide in their texts, ignoring the world as it changes around them. Even writing, however, is losing its reputation for trustworthiness. Writing increasingly seems a thing of the past; it can no longer be relied upon. Society, simultaneously, is losing its old foundations. The new world is represented by the suspect Troy, who is free of old convictions. In portraying the deceptive nature and decline of writing, Hardy begins to question the existence of the novel as a genre. Fiction seems to be just another comfort and deception; when Hardy abandons novel writing twenty years later, the truth of this seems to be confirmed.

Bibliography

Hardy, Thomas, *Far from the Madding Crowd* (London: Penguin, 1985).

Boumelha, Penny, *Thomas Hardy and Women: Sexual Ideology and Narrative Form* (New York: Prentice Hall, 1983).

Goode, John, *Thomas Hardy: The Offensive Truth* (Oxford: Blackwell, 1988)

Gregor, Ian, *The Great Web: The Form of Hardy's Major Fiction* (London: Faber & Faber, 1974)

1. Thomas Hardy, *Far from the Madding Crowd* (London: Penguin, 1985), p. 158. All further references are to this edition and are given parenthetically in the essay.

There is a lot to say about this essay. For example, the student writes with a real awareness of how to hold the attention of her audience. Even if you have never heard of *Far from the Madding Crowd*, you probably found you could understand and follow the essay. The student is writing with a sense of her reader needing to be led through the issue and looked after. An important aspect of this is the short opening paragraph, which sets up the subject of the essay, but does not stray into any unnecessary complications.

The case is then developed in six paragraphs, which are of roughly equal length. The end of paragraph 3 concludes one section of the essay, and the end of paragraph 5 concludes the next section. Paragraphs 6 and 7 then manage to raise the stakes, by finding a fresh dimension to the subject. The final paragraph, in a rather eloquent way, is then used to pull all the threads together and sum up. The result is an essay that is, simultaneously, simple and complex. It is simple in format, but builds a complex case. As we have stated, this might be an English Literature essay but the same organisational logic that drives this piece of work could drive an essay in any subject.

In this essay

1. Look at how each paragraph works very directly from small amounts of evidence.

2. Look at how nothing is asserted in advance of the evidence examined.

3. Look at how the essay – paragraph by paragraph – develops a case.

4. Look at how the student drives her case along.

5. Look at the care the student has taken over every detail of her essay (spelling, punctuation, grammar, layout, presentation, references).

▶ 65 How to get the first paragraph right

First paragraphs of essays are often far too ambitious. It is as if the writer has spent ages deciding what to say, and then pours it all out in a great torrent. What one also comes across is a great many essays that really have two opening paragraphs. The student introduces the topic, but in a paragraph that wanders round the issue; as that paragraph has not quite worked, the student decides to wander round the issue again in a second paragraph. Remember, at the start of an essay you should be attempting nothing more than to lead your reader into the subject. Write as if you are introducing them to the topic for the first time.

The first sentence always works best if it is a bold and direct statement. An essay might start as follows:

> In nearly two hundred years of history, the contribution made to the economy by British civil engineers has, by any reckoning, been inestimable.

But this is a cumbersome opening sentence. Try to make the opening as direct as possible:

> Civil engineers have made an invaluable contribution to the British economy.

It is the simple pattern we have stressed throughout this book: a sentence that follows the subject/verb/object (or complement) pattern in the most direct terms possible.

But where does one go after a striking opening sentence? Well, we have suggested that an essay works best if it falls into three distinct stages – with a beginning, a middle and an end – and it is possible to adopt the same approach when you are putting together a paragraph. In an opening paragraph:

- introduce the topic;
- expand or clarify that point;
- make it clear what the focus of the essay is going to be.

It is often the case that this three-step movement results in an opening paragraph of three sentences:

> Civil engineers have made an invaluable contribution to the British economy. Amongst engineers, it is Isambard Kingdom Brunel who has perhaps contributed most. His career, however, was characterised by a constant tension between his imaginative aspirations and hard economic realities.

If you consider the pattern of this paragraph, there is a topic sentence: the contribution of civil engineers. The second sentence advances matters, by singling out Isambard Kingdom Brunel. And then there is a third sentence that manages to define the true focus of the essay. It might be the case, of course, that you feel this is an appropriate opening strategy for some essays in some subjects, but that it has very little relevance to the challenges set in your subject. But the fact is that this structure always works. You are, in effect, talking to your reader. In three sentences, you say 'this is what I'm going to talk about', 'this in a little more detail is what I'm gong to talk about', and 'this is the problem, issue or question that I am going to confront in this essay'.

▶ 66 A strategy for every paragraph

Let us assume that you have managed to write a concise opening para-graph that gently introduces the subject matter of your essay to your reader. Each subsequent paragraph can then develop your considera-tion of the topic that you have identified. You might, for example, have been asked to write an essay about the popularity of astrology. In your first paragraph you might (i) explain what astrology is, (ii) point out how popular it is, and then (iii) pose the question about whether there is any substance to astrology.

Jot down your ideas. It makes sense to jot them down in three groups: the ideas you judge to be most basic, the more complex ideas, and the most difficult ideas. This will suit the pattern of an essay, where you advance from a simple beginning to a complex conclusion. Consequently, in an essay about astrology, you might, in the first third, focus on newspaper astrologers and fortune tellers. You might feel inclined to suggest that this is the most suspect aspect of astrology. Then, however, you might want to advance to consider just how much of a tradition there is to astrology, and that, even in the modern world, prominent people, including leaders of countries, have relied upon astrologers. But then you need to advance the argument. Consequently, in the last third of your essay you might broaden the issue out by thinking about the psychological implications of astrology: that astrologers tell people what they want to hear, and that they provide comfort and reassurance to people who are worried or facing enormous problems:

- 1   Introduction
- 2 and 3   Newspaper astrologers/fortune tellers
- 4 and 5   The tradition of astrology, and believers
- 6 and 7   Psychological explanations of the belief in astrology
- 8   Conclusion

Essentially, in contriving a strategy for each paragraph you should be dealing with your most straightforward (and easily handled) ideas as the essay begins, putting the next level of ideas in the middle of the essay, and keeping back your most difficult (and best) ideas for the last part of the essay.

Left to their own devices, most students embark upon their most difficult ideas almost immediately, probably because they sense that they are also their best ideas, but these ideas are squandered if they are used up too early in the essay. You need to start in a simple and direct fashion, and then try to make each paragraph in an essay just a little more ambitious than the paragraph before. In this way you can be seen to build your argument in rational, logical steps.

▶ 67 Making essay plans

A lot of students, at school, college and university, make an essay plan before they start to write. This is, of course, a good idea. But sometimes students make a rather shapeless list of all the points they want to cover in an essay, without thinking about the shape and form of the plan they are making. They jot down their ideas, listing them in the order they come to mind, and this list will probably dictate the form of the essay. What we are saying is to do it round the other way. Start with the form of the essay, with an essay template that encourages you to move the essay along from first principles to more complex implications.

What helps in doing this is to realise how many essay questions across the whole range of subjects actually ask very similar questions. If you were confronted by a question asking you to describe the record of the United Nations, and another question that asked you to consider the family in Britain today, your first instinct might be to say that there is absolutely no link between these two subjects. But, in fact, as with so many essay questions, they pose a problem about life and how we endeavour to control and organise life. The United Nations has, above all else, attempted to lessen international tension and the possibility of war. But the number of wars going on in the world at any one time draws attention to the near impossibility of the goal it has set itself. In a rather similar way, the family has traditionally been seen as providing structure and security in people's lives. But life today, with a rising divorce rate and changing standards of morality, has made the family a rather less robust unit than it used to be. Essentially, in writing about either of these topics you would be setting the factors in life that attempt to control events against the sheer complexity of life itself. In a way, writing an essay echoes this structure: your essay is confronting a complex problem, but the way in which it does so is by imposing the control of an organised essay on the diversity and complexity of the material you are examining.

But what has such an airy-fairy point about essay writing got to do with the actual activity of writing an essay? Well, one way of thinking about the structure of an essay is to see the three opening paragraphs as focusing on the elements of control. In paragraphs 4 and 5 you can then focus on the difficulty of the issues, problems or material that needs to be controlled. The final section of the essay can then negotiate some kind of solution: you might want to emphasise the success of the strategies of control, the partial success of the strategies of control, or the total failure of the strategies of control. If you were writing about the United Nations, for example, the first third of your essay might have focused on its role and function. The central part of the essay might have turned to the problems it has attempted to deal with. In the third part of the essay you might want to laud its success, say it has been a failure and irrelevant, or, most plausibly, talk about the fact that it has at times made a difference despite the impossibility of the role it has set itself.

So much of the strategy of essay writing involves seeing the issue behind the issue in this kind of way. For example, asked to discuss Shakespeare's play *Hamlet* as a tragedy, try to see that the use of the term 'tragedy' tries to pin down and define the play. The play itself, however, might well strike you as far more complex than the defining label. If that covered the first two stages of an essay, in the final section you would want to come to a conclusion about how useful, if at all, the term 'tragedy' is in describing a complex play. As with the essay about the United Nations, the most plausible answer is that the term 'tragedy' helps, but it does not cope with everything.

How do you recognise the elements of organisation and control implicit in a question? The strategy is to look very hard at the essay question itself. For instance, the kind of question that consists of a statement followed by the word 'discuss' offers you one person's attempt to pin down and make sense of a big issue. Your essay might well start by pursuing the concepts in the statement that constitute the question, showing how they do help us make sense of the subject under discussion. For example, the following question is from a Philosophy examination:

> 'The only time a human being is free is when he or she makes a work of art.'   (Friedrich von Schiller) Discuss.

To start with you would need to explain what this statement might mean, but by the middle of an essay you might be having some doubts about what is being said in the quotation. You might even be beginning to suspect that the statement is rather glib. By the end of the essay, however, you would need to move into a consideration of the role of art in life. It sounds very pretentious, but in fact the informing idea is the same as in any essay: the complex relationship between life and the structures we impose upon or create in order to manage and make sense of life.

▶ 68 The essay as a problem-solving device

What we have said so far might appear both reassuring and disturbing. We have suggested just how simple the structure of an essay can be, but we have also suggested that every essay you write touches in some way upon how people endeavour to comprehend and control the world and their lives. Don't worry about the more pretentious stuff in what we have written if you do not find that kind of thinking helpful. Concentrate, instead, on making a simple essay plan:

- 1   Introduction
- 2 and 3   The straightforward aspects of the question
- 4 and 5   Some of the more complicated implications
- 6 and 7   Where this gets us. This might involve a slightly more ambitious consideration of the relationship between the desire to comprehend and control life and the complexity of life.
- 8   Conclusion

But what also helps in making your basic essay plan is the knowledge that you do not have to solve problems in advance of writing an essay.

Indeed, one of the best ways of thinking about an essay is to see it as a problem-solving device. In the first paragraph, you ask the question. Then, working in a sequence of paragraphs of more or less the same length, you start to consider the issue. By the end of the first paragraph, you can say 'this is what I can say so far'. But there is, of course, more involved, so in the next paragraph you turn to the issue again, and then, a the end of the paragraph, you again state 'this is what I can say so far'. You need to keep on taking stock, seeing how your essay is advancing. This is one of the very good reasons for writing in paragraphs of roughly equal length. If you do not do this, there is a tendency to wander, to ramble and to get confused. But with regular paragraphs you can keep on taking regular breaks to consider how your answer is advancing. But the answers will not appear by magic. If you have posed a problem in the opening paragraph, you have to make sure that you create spaces in your essay where you take stock, seeing how your answer is shaping up. Do not make the mistake of leaving this to the very end of the essay. Keep on taking stock along the way. The place to do this is at the end of the paragraphs along the way.

▶ 69 The role of paragraph endings

All of us have been in that position where we do not know whether what we have written in an essay is any good or not. All of us have written essays where we are not quite managing to say what we are trying to say, or, perhaps even more commonly, where we are at something of a loss as to what it is we are trying to say. The easiest way of checking whether your essay is working, and also of introducing a greater element of control into a confused or confusing essay, is to take stock of your paragraph endings.

Immediate corrective surgery on an essay can be accomplished if you add one or two sentences at the end of each of the main paragraphs, sentences in which you attempt to stand back and sum up the case in your essay as it has developed up to that point. But this is more than a corrective measure. It is one of the fundamental secrets of essay writing: knowing that you have to keep on reasserting your control of the argument, and that the best place to do this is at the end of paragraphs. This is one of the times in essay writing where it helps to think very directly about your imagined reader. Imagine that you are writing about a complex subject, but trying to explain it to a younger brother or sister. You might read out your essay, but if you were thinking about this potential reader you would probably stop and say to them: 'So this is what I'm saying.' The point is that, if it helps to add this kind of commentary to the words in your essay when explaining the thinking in the essay to someone, it would probably improve the essay if you imported this extra degree of commentary and stock-taking into the essay itself.

This is where one of the advantages of writing an essay on a computer becomes very apparent. When you have written your essay, try tinkering with the end of each paragraph. It is easy to add and to delete sentences. You might well find that the addition of a couple of sentences at the end of some of the paragraphs along the way has a remarkable effect in terms of pulling your essay together. Suddenly it might be saying what you want it to say. And if you usually feel uncertain about the quality of your own work, you might be able to see that you are actually answering the question that has been set.

▶ 70 Troubleshooting

There are ten questions you might ask yourself.

Troubleshooting questions

1. Put yourself in the position of the reader of your essay. As the reader of the essay, do you understand it and do you find it persuasive?

2. Does the essay look logical and well organised? Is there a paragraph shape to the essay, or is it just a jumbled mixture of very short and very long paragraphs?

3. Is there a logical step-by-step advance in your essay?

4. Does the essay set up the issue efficiently and effectively?

5. Does each paragraph arrive somewhere?

6. Does each paragraph advance the argument?

7. Is the essay written in grammatical and properly punctuated sentences?

8. Does each sentence connect logically with the sentence that precedes and the sentence that follows it?

9. Would the essay benefit from cutting words and/or polishing and refining the expression of your ideas?

10. Does the essay conform to the conventions of presentation that are taken as standard in your subject or in the department where you are studying?

8 Essay Writing: Paragraph Control

▶ 71 The opening paragraph of an essay

At the heart of everything we have said about essay writing is the idea of thinking, organising and writing in three steps. An effective essay can – we would go so far as to say should – fall into three fairly distinct stages, in which you introduce the issue, pursue it and then, in the last third of the essay, take the matter a stage further. It is an equally good idea to aim for three steps in each paragraph of the essay. Later on in this section, we will discuss how this approach can be applied in the central paragraphs of an essay and in the conclusion, but what we want to focus on here is the opening paragraph of an essay.

The opening paragraph of any essay can be thought of as falling, almost naturally and inevitably, into three steps. The informing logic of this starts with what you are meant to be doing at this stage of an essay. You are introducing yourself to your reader and introducing your reader to the subject matter of your essay. As noted in the previous section, there is, understandably, a widespread impulse to write too much and to go on for too long in an opening paragraph. But you should try to resist this temptation. There is nothing to be gained from confusing the reader at the outset with too much information and too many ideas; all the reader requires is to be eased gently into the subject that is being discussed. In nearly all good essays, the first sentence is a fairly simple sentence. This can be thought of as the 'topic' sentence, in which, as concisely as possible, you indicate the subject matter of your essay. The second sentence (and, possibly, several sentences that will constitute the core of the paragraph) can then take up the challenge of the opening sentence, elaborating the issue and, where necessary, defining terms and providing the reader with essential information (but nothing more than essential information). The third step of the paragraph will be the closing sentence or sentences, which bring into focus as clearly as possible the brief of the essay, by which we mean the particular issue or problem that you are going to pursue in the broad topic under consideration.

Consider this example. The student had been set a question about the significance of feminism and postmodernism in late twentieth-century culture:

> **(i)** The latter years of the twentieth century can be associated with two 'isms': feminism and postmodernism. **(ii)** Feminism, committed to challenging the inherited order in society, was always, and overtly, political. By contrast, postmodernism can be regarded as a development in cultural and artistic history that favoured style over substance, and which, as such, shunned politics. **(iii)** But if we look a little more closely, it becomes apparent that the two movements overlap: that it is impossible to discuss postmodernism without considering political questions, and that, when we accept this fact, feminism and postmodernism can be seen as having a great deal in common.

Look closely at the structure of this paragraph. There is an opening sentence that, in a very uncomplicated way, establishes the broad topic of the essay. The paragraph then demands a couple of sentences in which there is an elaboration and clarification of the topic identified in the first sentence. Whatever topic you are called upon to discuss in an essay, you will always, after your opening sentence, have to clarify, elaborate and even define matters at this stage. But don't go on for too long, and don't make the mistake of just presenting facts. An essay focuses on a problem; the essay as a whole must amount to a case that you have argued. It is more important to establish the concepts, and some of their implications, than to plod wearily through, as this essay, for example, might have done, the entire story of twentieth-century feminism.

When you feel that you have offered the reader as much as is required in the way of elaboration, clarification and definition, you then need to move forward to a concluding step in the paragraph in which you start to indicate the aspects of the issue that your essay is going to concentrate upon. And that completes the three-step movement of an opening paragraph. It really can be, and perhaps always should be, as straightforward as this. What you also need to tell yourself is that an opening paragraph can, and should, be relatively short, perhaps no more than 10 to 12 lines in length. This relates to the aim of an opening paragraph, which is to introduce the reader to the topic. There is nothing to be gained from having a dense and enormously long opening paragraph if it provides your reader with more material than he or she can absorb at this early stage.

Your main priority in writing, both at the start and throughout your essay, should, indeed, be taking account of and looking after your reader. It is not your reader's job to work hard at understanding the essay; you have to do the hard work so that the reader can be led easily and clearly through the issue under discussion. At the outset, this is achieved best by a simple sequence of a topic sentence, followed by elaboration, clarification or definition, and then the final sentence of the paragraph decisively indicating the particular emphasis of the essay.

▶ 72 Write tight

You need to think about the shape of your opening paragraph, but you also need to ensure that you 'write tight'. What we mean by this should become apparent if you look at this opening paragraph for an essay on the figure of the fool in Shakespearean comedy and then compare it with a slimmer, tighter version of the same opening paragraph.

> As one of the longest running characters in theatre history, the part played by the fool has retained its significance due to the multiplicity of roles he performs within the dramas that he features in. He adopts a privileged position on stage as a character who is indirectly responsible for the guidance of the chief protagonists. However, his insight is seldom acknowledged by them and often even less respected. The reasons for this are what I intend to elucidate during the course of my essay which will examine the role of the Fool in *King Lear* and Feste in *Twelfth Night* who can be considered as perhaps two of Shakespeare's most dramatically complete fools. I will also address the way in which Bottom's function in *A Midsummer Night's Dream* can be interpreted as sharing the typical characteristics of an Elizabethan fool instead of the histrionic ramblings of a minor character.

As is so often the case in essays, what has been written doesn't quite work. Every sentence is just a little bit too loose and unfocused. Yet, as is so often the case in students' essays, what, at the moment, can only be considered rather poor work is only a short step away from becoming very good work.

What has gone wrong here is that the writer has not paid sufficient attention to the need for tightness and economy in writing. He could choose to start again, trying to write rather more tightly, or he could, as so often will be the case, make use of what initially has poured out as an untidy first draft, and fashion it into something tight and disciplined. In achieving this extra tightness, it helps immensely to keep on returning to our starting point, that a paragraph is, essentially, going through three steps – and that in rewriting a paragraph it is important to keep aware of these three steps. Suddenly, at this point, the unsatisfactory sprawl of a paragraph should become a thing of the past.

We identified the three steps in this paragraph, and then focused on producing a clearer topic sentence, a clear step of elaboration and definition, and then a clearer indication of the direction the essay will take. We have numbered these steps here, but obviously you would not number them in a final draft:

> **(i)** The fool performs a multiplicity of roles in Renaissance drama. **(ii)** Most obviously, he adopts a privileged position on stage as a character indirectly responsible for the guidance of the chief protagonists. However, they seldom acknowledge his insight. We can see this with the Fool in *King Lear* and Feste in *Twelfth Night*, who are two of Shakespeare's principal fools.
>
> **(iii)** But it is also interesting to consider Bottom, in *A Midsummer Night's Dream*, who, far from being just a histrionic minor character, can be seen to embody the typical characteristics of an Elizabethan fool.

What helps in this focusing of the paragraph is to bear in mind the basic sentence structure of subject/verb/object (or complement). Look at the opening sentence here: 'The fool [subject] performs [verb] a multiplicity of roles [object] in Renaissance drama.' All the sprawling messiness of the first draft has been eliminated by paying attention to two things: the standard shape of a paragraph, and the standard shape of a sentence.

▶ 73 Paragraph organisation

You need to think of three steps in a paragraph, and then present the paragraph in a disciplined way that conforms to the conventional rules of essay presentation. What we mean by this is nothing more complicated than making the effort to write in coherent paragraphs and grammatical sentences. What prompts us to say this is that a lot of students – perhaps particularly in science subjects, where the importance of a good essay technique might not be so obvious – are inclined to present their work in a format that resembles notes assembled for an essay rather than the essay itself.

Here are the opening sections of two science essays. One opening does not work; the second is successful. But the first opening is only a few steps away from working perfectly well; it is just that the student has not paid attention to the important concept of the architecture of his opening paragraph. As it is, he sprawls over several sentences, the sentences illogically appearing as separate paragraphs:

> A scientific method has been used since science began. It has played an extremely important role in the understanding of the Earth and the many things that occur within, on, and around it.
>
> In this essay I am going to discuss the scientific method by which data is analysed to produce a theory or to test a hypothesis in the Earth Sciences. The method will then be looked at in the other disciplines and similarities and differences will be discussed.
>
> The method consists of a number of steps that can be varied depending on the accuracy of the experiment to which it is applied. These include both practical and mental applications that hopefully produce a precise and relevant outcome when completed.
>
> This outcome can then be analysed further and applied in similar situations to that in which it was first found.

Because of the way in which this is written there is an impression of the essay, even at the outset, falling apart. But if just a little bit of attention had been paid to pulling these opening impressions together into the coherent package of a disciplined paragraph, then the essay would have got off to a good start.

This second student is rather more aware of how to get her essay off to a good start:

> In science it is commonly acknowledged that you cannot prove something to be right or true; you can only prove things to be false. You can, however, accumulate support for a theory by the repetition of logical scientific experiments. This is a process scientists must go through to establish a theory that will remain intact when held up to the scrutiny of their peers.

This is brief and to the point. There are three logical steps: the topic, elaboration of the topic, and an indication of the direction of the essay. The reader's attention has been caught. The impression is brisk and business-like.

It is at this point that you might want to ask questions and express reservations. Is it really possible to get away with such a short opening paragraph? Don't I need to say a lot more at the outset? Well, it depends. Your first consideration should be the needs of your reader: there is no point in bombarding you audience with too many facts and too much information. Just because you have included the information in your essay this does not mean that the reader has absorbed it. But in some essays you might feel it is essential to expand the middle section of the opening paragraph; you might want to define your concepts in some detail. But remember, you only need to elaborate to an extent that meets the needs of your audience.

▶ 74 Paragraph transitions: moving from paragraph to paragraph

You will often find that if you manage to get the first paragraph right, then everything else will fall into place as the essay develops. There is one very good reason why this could prove to be the case. A loose and sprawling opening paragraph has probably failed to make any really clear decision about the true subject matter of the essay. Aiming for concision at the outset and being aware of the architecture of the paragraph is likely to help in the business of seeing the central thread for the rest of the essay.

But there is a problem that often arises, even in very good essays, which is that there can be a disconcerting jolt from one paragraph to the next. There is a sense in which no logical connection is made. It would be possible, for example, to imagine that the opening paragraph of the poor science essay discussed above might be followed by a second paragraph that began as follows:

> Karl Popper was a philosopher whose main interest was in the philosophy of science and politics.

This, however, would be an abrupt and, seemingly, illogical move forward. The writer would probably – eventually – get around to noting that Popper had a great many interesting things to say about the scientific method, but the reader of the essay cannot be asked to wait for the connection in the argument to be made. The paragraph must follow on from the paragraph before, not make a fresh start.

What always needs to happen at the start of a paragraph is that it is essential to pick up one or more of the key words or issues from the paragraph before, and then to build from that point. It is a method that immediately establishes a sense of continuity – but it also establishes a sense of development. The impression, the correct impression, is that issues that have been touched upon are now going to be explored in greater detail. Look at the actual second paragraph of the good science essay that we praised in the previous unit and see how it picks up the thread from the first paragraph:

In science it is commonly acknowledged that you cannot prove something to be right or true; you can only prove things to be false. You can, however, accumulate support for a theory by the repetition of logical scientific experiments. This is a process scientists must go through to establish a theory that will remain intact when held up to the scrutiny of their peers.

It is sometimes convenient to take for granted that theories are true. This creates a base on which new theories and predictions can be formulated. Newton's Laws of Motion are an example of this. Newton devised these laws in the eighteenth century and they were universally considered an accurate portrayal of the behaviour of mass in movement. However, now that man has the ability to accelerate matter close to the speed of light, it can be seen that matter only observes Newton's Laws of Motion at relatively small speeds. Although Newton's laws have been revised to work in relation to near-light speeds, the original laws are still used when considering slower speeds.

The first paragraph foregrounded truth and falsity as interesting propositions in science. The second paragraph has recognised that it might be a good idea to take up, and pursue, one of those terms. It thus picks up the word 'true' and makes it serve as a link between the paragraphs.

The transition the student makes from her second to her third paragraph is equally effective:

An alternative view, strongly held by the philosopher Karl Popper, is that the true aim of an experiment is to disprove, not prove, a prediction: 'If a a scientist attempts to predict surprising results from her theory (if she attempts to falsify it) and fails, this provides even more powerful verification for the theory.' Scientific knowledge is built on observations that can be supported by logical, systematic experiments. These experiments aim to be repeatable and to produce identical results in laboratories worldwide. To allow results to be repeatable there is a 'scientific method' that all experiments follow. The majority of experiments spring from observations. As a result of these observations a hypothesis can be formed. 'A hypothesis is a supposition made as the basis of reasoning or investigation' (Oxford Dictionary, 1996). Most hypotheses rely on laws that allow predictions to be made.

It is the phrase 'An alternative view' that enables us to see how successfully this essay is moving from one paragraph to the next. Implicit in the phrase 'An alternative view' is the idea that one idea has been expounded, but now it is time to move on to the next idea. It is, however, one that relates to what has gone before, even if it relates to it by being the opposite of that proposition.

It is this kind of simple sign-posting that is needed at the end and beginning of paragraphs. Implicitly you are saying, 'Well, we have come along this route so far, this is where we are now, and this seems to be the best direction in which to move forward.' It is a good idea in writing an essay if you can create polished versions of these transition sentences as the essay is being written. There's a simple mental process involved: you ask yourself, 'What have I said so far?', which should then help you define what you need to consider next. It often helps if the opening sentence of a paragraph includes a word such as 'therefore' or 'however'. The word 'therefore' suggests that there is more to be said on the point that has been raised, whereas 'however' suggests that it is now time to look at the same issue from a different angle. But both serve the same function of establishing a link from one paragraph to the next.

In an ideal world, we would, of course, always write these transition words or phrases that knit the argument together as we were writing the first draft of the essay. But the fact is that these transition sentences – the ones that close and open paragraphs – are likely to acquire their final shape only in the final stages of putting together the final version of the essay. More often than not, students produce essays where they are almost in control of the argument. If, just before handing an essay in, you feel that your essay isn't quite working, then this is the point at which you need to tinker with paragraph endings and openings. Because this is the last stage in refining an essay, however, we will return to this stage of the polishing process at the end of this section.

▶ 75 Constructing paragraphs (1)

The opening paragraph of an essay is both the easiest and most diffi-cult to put together. It is the easiest because it can afford to be fairly short, and is just introducing the topic in a way that should be as uncomplicated as possible. But the opening paragraph is also difficult to write as you are having to think about the subject as a whole. An essay can work as a problem-solving device, but you can't really get things under way until you have got the measure of the problem in some form.

Subsequent paragraphs in the essay should then be devoted to discussing the issue as you have defined it in your opening paragraph. Everything possible can go wrong in putting these paragraphs together: they can turn out to be chaotic, irrelevant, and illogical. What you need is a way of thinking and working that guards against this. What we suggest is that, as in your first paragraph, you think in three steps. But you might also think about three steps within three steps. Let us suppose that you had been asked to write about the strengths and weaknesses of Bill Clinton as the President of the United States. Your opening paragraph might have (a) said that Clinton was the president, (b) said those were good years for America, and (c) asked to what extent he could take the credit.

In paragraph 2, you might think in terms of a link sentence – that we can see many good qualities in Clinton as president. You then elaborate, and then, at the end of the paragraph, try to reach a running conclusion. There are, therefore, three steps. But to achieve some real weight in the paragraph, you might want, in the elaboration section of the paragraph, to pick out three related good qualities. You might, for example, decide to concentrate on his personal qualities: saying that (a) he seemed to have an ability to get on well with everyone – that Americans liked him, (b) he was particularly popular with black American voters, and (c) he got on well with the British prime ministers John Major and Tony Blair. The paragraph might end by saying that such personal qualities might seem trivial, but they certainly account for some of his success as a president.

In paragraph 3, you might then deal with how his human qualities were also a problem, as in his relationship with Monica Lewinsky. For example:

> The human qualities that brought Clinton such success, however, were also responsible for his downfall. His affair with Monica Lewinsky can be seen as part of the same charismatic attraction that he had for the American people. Here was a man who drew others to him but who also used his personal charm and good looks to further his own desires. The affair damaged Clinton personally, but also underlined how fragile his political credo was. A policy based on charisma and human warmth is always liable to go off course or to be blown astray by emotions, unlike sticking to a steady plan of government. This was the case in the Lewinsky affair where Clinton allowed his emotions to overrule his reason.

Thinking about the shape of the rest of the essay, paragraphs 4 and 5 might focus on the success of his policies – how he (4) achieved a lot internationally and (5) presided over boom years in the American economy. But 6 and 7 could then turn round to argue that events shape politicians, rather than politicians shaping events: that the problems in Ireland and Israel, for example, were beyond solution, and (7) that the economy might have a life of its own which politicians cannot affect. As always, it is simplicity of format that one is looking to achieve in an essay.

The relevant point here, however, is the format and content of the main paragraphs during the course of the essay. What we are suggesting is three steps – but then also three main points in the central bit of each of these paragraphs.

▶ 76 Constructing paragraphs (2)

Someone once said that modern novels consist of a beginning, a muddle and an end. When essays go wrong, this is how they go wrong – most of the paragraphs along the way get into an awful muddle. All that is needed to avoid this is a certain amount of thought about the architecture of each paragraph in the main body of the essay.

Your opening paragraph should have established the issue or problem that is being looked at. It is worth repeating a fundamental point here. A good essay will have a narrative shape, in that it develops a kind of story, but you aren't just presenting a narrative of events in an essay. An essay is examining or discussing a problem. The essay as a whole amounts to a clear argument that you construct from evidence. In each of the main paragraphs you need to establish the next step of your argument.

The three-part structure of a paragraph should help you do this. The opening sentence establishes the topic for the paragraph. The last sentence (in a way that we consider in the next unit) pulls the threads of the paragraph together. In the middle of the paragraph you need to start producing your evidence. Think of yourself as a barrister in court. Your essay might be on the origins of the First World War. Your first paragraph would probably have established that the causes were complex and various. In the second paragraph you would have started by saying, for example, that there was a record of instability in the Balkans, and that we can see this in. . . . The paragraph will begin to take shape and feel really substantial if you can provide three brief, relevant examples of this political instability. Paragraph 3 might consider the years just before 1914. But then in paragraphs 4 and 5 you would probably want to move on to a larger issue, of international tension between Germany and the other major powers.

But the point is that in the body of the paragraph there needs to be evidence – and evidence that is not presented as 'this happened and then this happened', but evidence that is presented in the manner of proving a case in court: consider this, and consider this, and consider this. Where this is all leading you is towards the final sentence of the paragraph, which is a temporary or running conclusion of the essay in which you more or less say that, if we take account of all the evidence so far, what we have to conclude is, for example, that the origins of the war go beyond the immediate years of 1914 and involve a huge power struggle in Europe about unresolved political issues.

And then the same paragraph building has to go on in paragraphs 6 and 7. These might be concerned with arguing how the origins of the war go back even further, that they lie in a long-running battle over territory and national identity in the region. But don't just assert such points; present the evidence that underlies the case. And then, in the final part of paragraph 6, use the end to draw the evidence together, saying where it gets us. Similarly with paragraph 7: set out your opening sentence, and then provide the evidence or analysis that will allow you to reach a conclusion. So much of paragraph discipline is having this sense of how each paragraph works to build the essay, and how the same basic structure underlies each paragraph.

▶ 77 Paragraph endings

The essence of what we are saying is that it is possible to have a formulaic pattern – a sense of the shape of an essay – that underlies anything you write. Far from cramping what you might want to say, this kind of disciplined structure is actually liberating. It enables you to say far more than you knew you could say, and probably will enable you to surprise yourself with the force and originality of what you can argue. The pattern in the main paragraph is

- link sentence;
- evidence produced – if possible, three pieces of evidence;
- a conclusion reached.

At the moment we are focusing on how to build an essay along those lines, but in the next section of this book we will, in a sense, present the process in reverse, showing you how to break down what you know into a three-step essay with three steps to each paragraph, and three steps of evidence in each paragraph.

The fact is that when students start to see the logic of this approach, they take to it very quickly and their essays almost immediately start getting better marks. But there is one area even in this scheme of things that lots of students find difficult – which is knowing just how to end a paragraph. What you really need to do here is to take stock, to sum up the case so far. The difficulty most students experience is that they are never entirely clear what it is that they have managed to establish in the course of the paragraph. The problem is that they need to stand back and be reflective, but because this is quite hard to do they characteristically engage in tactics that enable them to avoid doing so. For example, they might simply end with the evidence, without summing up the evidence. Or they might slide into material that really belongs in the next paragraph.

The answer is to tell yourself that you absolutely must have at least one, and possibly two or three sentences at the end of each of the main paragraphs that sum up the case so far. Look at this sample paragraph:

> Language, as we have seen, enables us to a do a multitude of tasks. It helps us to communicate ideas and points as well as to describe dreams and emotions. It helps us to organise our world by placing certain structures on the daily business of life through such things as newspapers, books, diaries and even emails with all their irregular spellings and grammar. Above all, it enables us to think about the past and the future so that we can plan the shape of our existence in a meaningful pattern by labelling days of the week, seasons and, most obvious of all, months and years. These multiple features of language give it a central place in our activity; they point to language as the key to human life.

One way of thinking about this is to have a very clear idea of an audience for your essay. As noted in the previous section, you might think in terms of your mum or dad, or a younger brother or sister. And then, more or less, but not in colloquial language, write on the lines of 'Look mum, this is what it's all about, this is what I'm on about.' Really, you are in a more explicit way providing a running commentary on what you have written – but it works best if the running commentary actually finds a place in the essay itself. In our experience, when we are returning essays to students, if we ask what they were trying to argue in a particular paragraph, they can usually provide an articulate impression of what they had in mind. But they didn't write it down at the end of the paragraph, possibly because it involved committing themselves. An essay isn't going to build and advance unless you consciously add to and advance your overall case in this kind of way.

▶ **78 The final third of an essay**

In an ideal essay, the opening paragraph raises a problem, and then, just a handful of paragraphs later, your reader should be amazed at how professionally and persuasively you have analysed and discussed that problem. This necessarily involves each paragraph advancing your examination of the issue. But as we have already said in this book, in order for an essay really to sparkle the essay needs to acquire fresh energy, and perhaps a fresh direction, in the last third. Characteristically, the opposite tends to happen; essays that start promisingly run out of steam about two-thirds of the way through. It is as if the student can see that the argument should be heading in a rather more adventurous direction, but can't find that direction and so more or less gives up, and simply treads water, repeating (perhaps in a slightly different form) points that have already been made.

In order to get some extra zip in the last third of an essay, there are some essay-writing strategies that you can call upon. The most important one is that two-thirds of the way through (that's at the end of paragraph 5 in an eight-paragraph essay) you really need to take stock in a decisive and extended manner. What you really are saying is 'I've looked at the evidence and this is where, when I piece all this together, I have arrived.' Consider this example:

> The argument thus far has been that *Julius Caesar* is a play about a power struggle that begins with celebration of Caesar's recent victory but soon turns into the political problem of how to act in the face of an apparent threat to Rome's constitution. Caesar, it seems, will become king and the established hierarchy of senators, tribunes and people will be overthrown. More, the freedom Brutus values so dearly, along with the main aspects of Rome, will be lost. Immediately after the murder, as I noted above, the conspirators wish to make it known that they have restored 'Liberty, freedom, and enfranchisement'. In this way the play is self-evidently concerned with large political concepts and issues. Indeed, there can be little doubt that *Julius Caesar* is a play that examines both the language and violence of politics in an intensely dramatic way.

Really you are saying, at the end of the paragraph, 'That's what it all amounts to, now where do we go from here?'

It might be, for example, that this sets you up for a last third of the essay that starts with an implied 'But', as if you are going to challenge the drift of everything you have said so far. But the real point is that your almost exaggerated taking stock at the end of paragraph 5 has cleared the details so that you can see what hasn't yet been considered. In the case of our essay on *Julius Caesar*, for example, paragraph 6 might go on to suggest not simply that the play is dramatic but that there is something deliberately theatrical about politics in Rome. This comes out in Mark Antony's address to the crowd following Caesar's death where he is able to use the cloak as prop to manoeuvre the crowd's sympathy. The same theatricality is present when we first see Caesar and in the image he promotes of his being unlike other men and not subject to their failings. Such theatricality is concerned with the outward show of things. Paragraph 7 might take this point up and argue that underlining the play is the sense of a world in which politics is enmeshed in display and open to constant misinterpretation. The conspirators may proclaim 'Freedom, liberty, and enfranchisement', but their arms are dipped up to the elbows in blood. In this way they seem to embody the political contradictions and tensions of the play.

But there are other directions in which paragraphs 6 and 7 on *Julius Caesar* might go. The point to grasp is that if the previous paragraphs have done their work, and in particular if at the end of paragraph 5 you have taken stock and really pulled the essay together, then you can move the essay forward with a good deal of confidence. You will know that you have laid all the solid foundations of the essay and set out a series of pieces of evidence that have brought you to a certain kind of conclusion. Now you can consider something new and really push your luck.

▶ 79 Moving from paragraph to paragraph

These are some of the steps in paragraph control that we have dealt with so far in this section:

- A clear opening paragraph, in 3 steps, that introduces the topic, elaborates and defines it, then specifies the problem
- Main paragraphs that start with a linking topic sentence, that then turn to evidence, and then reach a conclusion
- If possible, three chunks of evidence in each paragraph
- This will lead to a conclusion – which we discuss in the next unit.

If you write an essay along these lines, there is a very good chance that you will feel that you are in control of your material, in control of the issue being discussed, and in control of the essay. Characteristically, however, even at this stage, students feel that their essay needs pulling together in some way. It is a very common feeling that the essay, by this stage, is almost, but not quite doing the job required. If the basic architecture of your essay is as it should be (which means that it follows the kind of pattern we have just outlined), we can tell you with total confidence how to fine-tune your essay so that it does acquire that final degree of control you are seeking.

What you need to focus on is the closing sentences of paragraphs and the opening sentences of paragraphs. The method we have been recommending has stressed the importance of a shape, a direction and overall development of an essay. But sometimes it is quite late in the day before you realise what it is that your essay has managed to prove. Indeed, there is every possibility that as you have put so much energy into making the essay work at all, you didn't have time to see where it was all leading and what it all amounts to. But if you tinker with the opening and ends of paragraphs, that will provide the extra tightness. Indeed, one key way of polishing an essay to ensure that it holds together and flows is to think of adding twelve extra sentences to pull the whole essay together.

Such sentences need not be particularly stylish or complicated. Here are three examples of opening and closing sentences that can be used in this way. The first sentence at the start of a paragraph is designed to link back to the previous paragraph while the concluding sentence ensures that the paragraph has arrived somewhere:

first: The evidence considered so far . . .
last: All of this suggests . . .

first: The argument so far . . .
last: What this points to . . .

first: This, however, is not the whole answer . . .
last: In sum, the evidence confirms that . . .

In each case the sentence serves to draw the argument of the essay together to ensure that it is tightly structured. It is a matter of standing back and making sure you point up the connections between paragraphs and draw out the implications of the evidence you offer.

▶ 80 Writing a conclusion

Lots of people have problems writing conclusions. They do not know what to say and they do not know how much to say. The first thing to remember is that the conclusion is the conclusion. It is not the point at which to start introducing fresh evidence or additional stages in the argument. Sometimes students start saying all the things they should have said in running conclusions along the way. The main problem students experience, however, is that they find themselves writing conclusions that they know are dull. They are dull because they are summing up all the steps of the argument they have constructed. What they need to be doing is saying what it is that they know now that they did not know when they wrote the first paragraph of the essay. They need to force the attention onto what the essay has uncovered. And this can be done in a paragraph that is as short and straightforward as the opening paragraph.

Look at this example:

> Bill Clinton may not go down in history as the greatest president ever. His personal life tends to overshadow his attempts to resolve international and economic problems that always seem to be with us. But his charismatic warmth gave politics a new lease of life and also gave people a new sense of hope that politicians do care. In this he restored something of the human touch to the grand abstractions that make up government.

There are three simple steps here: the issue restated / the new thesis that has been advanced / a declaration of the new position reached. A conclusion can, and should, be as simple as this. The hard work, and hard argument, has been done in the main paragraphs of the essay; the final paragraph is just a clear statement of what you know now that you didn't know before.

And that should be the end of the matter – but it isn't quite. Even as you finish you should make time to check that your essay has been properly written. Here is a checklist of five key points about paragraph control:

Paragraph checklist

1. Is the opening paragraph of the essay direct and clear?

2. Do your paragraphs advance the case being made?

3. Do your paragraphs link together?

4. Do your paragraphs arrive somewhere?

5. Does your concluding paragraph point out what the essay has uncovered?

9 Make Every Essay an Effective Essay

► 81 **What are they looking for?**

When you are asked to write an essay, you are, of course, being tested. The test falls into two complementary parts. The people examining your work want to establish whether you have taken possession of the kind of knowledge and understanding of the topic that is consistent with the standard they are demanding. In simple terms, a university course would demand more in the way of knowledge and understanding than a GCSE course in the same subject. It is the lectures, discussions, seminars and the books recommended for reading that alert you to the level of sophistication and depth of understanding that is required at each stage of your education.

But there is an additional level in assessment, a second thing you are being tested on. You are being tested on your ability to analyse and synthesise the material you have been taught, and whether you can present this in the form of a written answer. In other words, the process starts with knowledge and understanding, but you are also being evaluated on the skills you display in providing a demonstration of your knowledge and understanding. To a large extent, the skills involved remain the same whatever subject you are studying; in particular, an ability to communicate clearly is fundamental in any piece of written work. This, in effect, means writing sentences in grammatically correct English. But there are also other qualities that will be rated as particularly important in specific subjects. Most students are unaware of the fact, but at every level, from GCSE through A-level and up to graduate and postgraduate degrees at university, there are criteria of assessment, in which the people setting your examination papers have to state in quite precise terms what they are looking for and what particular qualities they will reward. The chances are that you have been issued with the criteria of assessment for the courses you are taking at the moment; you probably dismissed them as bumph that was not worth reading, but there is a great deal to be said for looking closely at the qualities called for and how they are described. An hour spent reading the criteria could provide a much clearer focus and direction for your written work.

Mind you, a lot of what is said is blindingly obvious; if, for example, you are studying the reign of King Henry VIII in history, you could probably guess in advance that you are not going to be asked a question that asks you to describe his favourite food. That might be interesting, but it is trivial information with no intellectual substance in it. In a way, you know even before you start the course that you are going to be asked about his conduct as king, his success, or lack of success, in leading the country, and about the relationship between England and other countries (Wales, Scotland and Ireland, and countries on the continent) during his reign. In a rather similar way, a medical student knows before starting the course that if there is a question about possible treatments for a certain disease, then advocating the power of crossing one's fingers as the most effective remedy will not result in a very good mark. What we are saying is that a combination of common sense and the briefest acquaintance with a subject should provide the most substantial indication of what is expected in essays and examinations.

Common sense will also tell you that an essay question will, in all likelihood, be asking you to consider a problem. There will not be all that many questions where you are asked simply to describe something. For example, in an Education degree, you are unlikely to be asked to provide a brief history of comprehensive schools, but you are very likely to be asked to consider the advantages and disadvantages of a system of comprehensive schools. Even if the question confronts the student with a problem, however, there will be some students who simply provide a narrative account of the history of comprehensive schools, rather than tackling the problem they have been asked to discuss. Don't fall into this trap; make sure that you are always constructing an argument. All the advice we have presented in these chapters on essay writing has been about how to build an effective argument.

This will be the broad strategy of your answer, to offer an effective argument that addresses the problem in the question set. Then, make sure you have read the criteria in order that you are alert to any particular qualities that are being demanded in your chosen subject. But, then, as a final point make sure that you are alert to, and pay close attention to, any specific conventions that those teaching you insist upon. To provide a small, but highly relevant, example: one university department we know provides students with detailed advice about how students must cite and acknowledge the books they have read and the texts they have quoted from. In the first year, about half of the students make a real effort to follow this guidance, but half the class, initially, ignore the advice. Essays are then returned to students with a mark as follows: MARK 62 MINUS 5 FOR POOR PRESENTATION ACTUAL MARK 57. That difference of five marks represents the difference between a good degree result and a merely average degree result in the UK.

You will not be surprised to hear that students in this department soon become highly proficient in complying with the department's presentation conventions. Other departments might not be as transparent in penalising students, but the fact is that your department will have conventions. These will have been conveyed to you in a students' handbook and it is your responsibility to comply with these conventions. If you fail to do so, someone, somewhere, will be deducting marks. The best response to this, as you might expect, is to take that little bit of extra care in the way you present your essay so that it becomes self-evident that you have planned it and know what you are doing. The rest of this section is about such planning. It draws on points raised in earlier sections, pulling them together in an overarching view of the various essay-writing exercises that can be set and offering you advice about how to manage your assessments.

▶ 82 Planning and preparation

It should be clear from everything said so far in this book that when you write an essay you should be seeking to produce the best argument you can, and in accordance with the criteria and conventions specified in the subject you are studying. But it's worth stopping here first to consider the work that can be done, and has to be done, before an essay is written. The best advice we can offer is to say that when you are doing preparatory work, make sure that it is the right kind of preparatory work, specifically in terms of preparing for the essay that you should be writing. Teachers usually set a word limit. That should be your starting point; as you prepare an essay plan you should be thinking about how much material you need in order to conform with that word limit. You will lose marks if your essay is too long.

It is at this point that some students complain that they had so much to say that they found it impossible to keep to the word limit. But, in claiming this, they are in fact admitting that they have misunderstood the nature of the assessment exercise they are doing. They are suggesting that the essay or examination is merely a test of knowledge and understanding, whereas what is also being tested is the student's ability to present an argument in a well-organised essay. Students who write too much are revealing that they lack the ability to select and edit their own work and to control their writing. You must ensure that what you offer in an answer conforms to what the department is asking for. In fact, many departments will take a harsh line on work that is too long. A student can be forgiven for finding a subject difficult and, therefore, for struggling to produce a good essay, but there is no reason to forgive someone who cannot understand the concept of a word limit.

Beyond such obvious advice, however, how does one set about planning and preparing an essay? The best approach is to start with a clear idea of the number of paragraphs you intend to have in the essay; we have talked about eight-paragraph essays so far, but other sensible formats (as we will explain in the course of this section) are 11 paragraphs and 20 paragraphs. Then try to slot what you want to say into this pre-determined plan. There is, of course, another method, which is to start jotting down what you want to say, and the different points you want to make, but this method can be terribly unrewarding, as your plan is likely to sprawl without finding any particular shape. Some people suggest using spider-web diagrams or coloured flow charts for different points and ideas, but these methods can quickly run out of shape. It makes much more sense, and is far more productive, if you attempt to fit what you want to say into a predetermined essay format. We are not saying here, 'don't bother with having adventurous and interesting ideas' – that would be foolish advice. Essays are, after all, about ideas, but they don't have to be planned as if they were going to be hung in the Tate Gallery. The topic and scope of an essay can be as diverse as you want, but that makes it all the more sensible to think in terms of a neat, logical, step-by-step essay plan that you are going to slot your material into.

▶ 83 The three-step plan

One way of tackling an essay is to work out your argument in great detail in advance, but it is also possible to use the kind of eight-paragraph structure we have been describing here as a problem-solving device. This is something we touched on in Section 7 where we also discussed essay planning and how to use your knowledge of how to organise an essay to help you build an argument. You need only be aware of your point of departure, and you can then use the format – the sequence of steps in the essay – to lead you through the issue so that you can arrive at an answer. It takes a bit of nerve to write in this way, but it really does work. You cannot do it, however, unless you think of an essay as a series of steps in which, in a predetermined way, you have decided in advance what will, in general terms, be happening at each stage of the essay.

Step One is the first paragraph where you state the problem. At this stage you don't know the answer but you begin to work it out. The easiest way of doing this is to think in terms of three moves. In the first sentence you state the topic the essay is dealing with. You then elaborate on the topic so that it has more substance and content; and in the third move you pull the paragraph together in a concluding sentence. The first paragraph thus sets the essay up with something to discuss. Paragraphs 2 and 3 then fill out the topic but also arrive at conclusions. By the end of paragraph 3 you should have done your initial assessment of the topic problem.

Step Two takes in paragraphs 4 and 5 of the essay. This is where the essay will make sure that it has covered the issue in a solid fashion, working in details that support the argument but also that lead it forward. Notice that we don't want to include details for their own sake but rather for how they help us shape and identify the main line of the argument. As in Step One, make sure each paragraph reaches a conclusion that develops the argument.

Step Three is paragraphs 6 and 7. Here you look for the complication in the argument. The easiest way of thinking about this is to see the opening steps as taking the essay in a certain direction, but then in this third stage to spot another level to the problem. And then, finally, round off the essay with paragraph 8. Like the opening paragraph, this can be relatively brief, drawing together your ideas but without going over the whole essay again.

An example: You have been set an essay asking you to consider the relationship between popular Hollywood films and the cult of violence. The question seems to be asking whether films glamorise violence. Your essay frame can help you start to sort out an answer:

Step One is to state the problem: that many Hollywood films seem to glamorise violence. Films like *Rambo* and *Reservoir Dogs* seem to share a common language of violence, though it is far from clear if they reflect everyday life. This is paragraph 1. Then, in paragraphs 2 and 3, you start to fill out the case, looking at *Rambo* and the images of violence it presents. But the case needs to arrive somewhere: that, for example, *Rambo* seems to glamorise military violence and masculinity at the expense of the social order,

Step Two is paragraphs 4 and 5. The essay here needs to incorporate some more details. This might come in the form of looking at a second film such as *Reservoir Dogs*. Paragraph 4 might be about the use of blood imagery in *Reservoir Dogs*, while paragraph 5 might concentrate on the slayings in the film. In each case, though, the paragraphs need to advance the argument: that the exaggeration of violence takes it away from the mundane world into fantasy; that cult movies are a different matter from the cult of violence and belong to a recognisable genre.

Step Three comprises paragraphs 6 and 7. Here you can push the case on, using other examples of films that exploit violence in a recognisably formulaic way. Or you might turn the argument back against itself with a new level to the problem: that, for example, violent films, though they may not reflect the everyday, may offer images which reinforce patterns or ideas of violence, especially against women. Your final paragraph can then suggest that films and society may interact in troubling and disturbing ways in terms of gender and violence.

What initially holds the essay together is the shape you bring to it. In turn this allows you to begin working out an answer, but using a series of three steps or stages in the way described also gives the essay a line of argument that takes it forward. That is really the key point: you are never simply being asked to write an essay but always are required to build an analytical argument.

▶ 84 The longer essay

The advice above might seem so obvious as to be unnecessary. After all, don't all books tell you to write in paragraphs? They do, but they rarely explain why, or why it is so useful to you and your reader. Nor do they really grasp how to make the essay structure do the work for you. Your template guarantees in advance that your essay has a shape and design. In practical terms, having an essay method means you know where your essay is going and what you are seeking to achieve. In effect, you are driving the essay rather than allowing the essay to go where it wants.

We have suggested above that you might start an essay with only the most general sense of the argument and then use the three-stage plan to develop it. But you might prefer (and in some subjects it might make more sense) to work out more of the issue in advance of writing the essay, especially if you have to write a longer essay than the 1500 to 2000-word essay we have been discussing. Whereas that kind of word limit can usefully be seen in terms of 8 paragraphs, a longer essay naturally falls into more paragraphs. But you don't want to construct an essay that has a string of small paragraphs just because the word limit is higher. Nor do you really want to opt for increasing the size of your paragraphs. Two-thirds or three-quarters of a page is long enough for a decent paragraph and also lets your reader see where the writing is going. If short paragraphs destroy any sense of continuity, long paragraphs lose force and focus. For this reason we suggest that for an essay of between 2000 and 3000 words you think in terms of 11 paragraphs.

Once again a three-step plan helps. How? Let us assume you have been set any topic. In your first paragraph you state the topic, and try to divide that subject into three parts. But what do we mean by three parts? There is no simple, correct answer. If, for example, the topic was 'Abortion' you might decide to say there are arguments for and against, and a third 'in some cases' view. But that's only one option. You could divide it into the legal view, the religious and moral view, and, finally, the woman's perspective. Or any three that suit you. Take some time over it. But can you see how organisation is being established in your essay? The three parts of the subject will then form the basis of the three steps in your essay as you deal with each in turn.

An example: you have been asked to write an essay of 2500 words on abortion. This is a hugely emotive subject and one that embraces a large set of issues. But you cannot cover everything; you have to choose. In your initial thinking you decide to divide the topic into the legal, the ethical and the human aspects.

Paragraph 1   introductory sentence stating the topic
the three aspects of the problem
a final sentence to round off the paragraph

Step One – paragraphs 2, 3 and 4

Step Two – paragraphs 5, 6 and 7

Step Three – paragraphs 8, 9 and 10

Paragraph 11   conclusion

This slightly longer essay plan emphasises even more plainly than everything we have said so far the logic of essay writing. The structure provides the framework in which to explore ideas, but it is a framework that allows the argument to develop, moving from straightforward material in the opening stage, through material in the middle stage that grounds the essay in solid detail, and on to a final stage where a more nuanced or complex approach can emerge as you push deeper into the subject, exploring some of its more problematic, contradictory aspects as you build your case. Thus, while the law on abortion may be reasonably clear, though not without its opponents, and while the ethical debate about termination has been carefully articulated by both pro- and anti-lobbyists, the human dimension of the issue seems fraught with difficulties for all, but especially women.

Even a bare outline such as this of the steps in the argument suggests how the essay can be developed and researched. The starting point, though, is seeing how stating the topic and dividing it into three aspects provides a lead into the rest of the essay.

▶ 85 **Reports**

Most of us are familiar with school reports, but there are also government reports on almost every aspect of public life, company reports from businesses, reports on major accidents and special reports dealing with complex legal or moral matters. The world is, in fact, full of reports of one kind or another and report writing is a useful skill to develop. By their very nature reports need to be orderly, but also analytic. The three-step method we have used throughout this book provides a way to manage these tasks with confidence and clarity. In the case of reports, however, we suggest that you opt for three numbered sections (I, II, III) to set out the three key areas of the report so as to give the document that necessary sense of formality.

The real advantage of the three-section plan is that it means you know what you are doing from the word go. Even as you start to read for your report, you can begin to sift and sort your material, looking out for points and details that play an important part in the report. Instead of simply collecting endless data and then having to arrange it in some kind of order that makes sense to the reader, here you already know the order and can judge accordingly where material best belongs. A report on conservation, for example, might well begin with legislation, then move on to the challenges posed by greenhouse warming before turning, finally, to forecasts and possible action plans. Can you see how, even before a word of the report is written, the analysis has begun? Instead of having to work through all the material a second time to order it, you exploit the advantages of the report framework.

But the framework is also flexible enough to allow for change and unexpected findings: each section has a three-paragraph structure where precisely these things can be introduced. For example, section II on greenhouse warming might begin with an overview of where knowledge is, then, in the next paragraph, look at contrary findings that argue against the greenhouse effect, but then, in the third paragraph, highlight current research in a specific area that puts the problem in a new light. As with all writing, reports are a matter of letting the structure do a great deal of the work for you so that you can see the implications of what you are saying and focus on the important points.

Of course, reports are not always the most exciting of documents, and certainly you would do well to curb your sense of humour when writing them since shafts of wit are always liable to be misunderstood. A jokey report on a football club that has lost millions of pounds will not impress fans or investors. On the other hand, there is no reason why reports should not be readable, informative and well written. Indeed, they are likely to be much more use if they are well organised and carefully written. But what matters most in a report is the confident control over the material. Such control provides the reader with a clear path so that its content can be absorbed and understood quickly and easily:

Introduction: paragraph 1
    an introductory sentence stating the topic,
    the three aspects of the report using three sentences,
    a final sentence to round off the paragraph.

Section I – paragraphs 2, 3 and 4,

Section II – paragraphs 5, 6 and 7

Section III – paragraphs 8, 9 and 10

Conclusion – paragraph 11

It should be evident that this framework will allow you to produce between 2000 and 3000 words without overburdening your reader. It provides sufficient space to explore major points and weigh up the evidence involved. But it also forces you to concentrate the report on important items rather than endlessly listing bullet points and adding so many details that the report becomes shapeless and unmemorable. In the conclusion you may well wish to summarise the findings of the report. In some cases you may be asked to do so in a separate summary or in the Introduction. (Very formal reports, such as legal reports, may begin with Recommendations, followed by Introduction, Findings, and Conclusions.) These, however, are minor points: what is expected of you in a report is a combination of information and analysis, not a maze of points that lack coherence or direction.

▶ 86 Longer essays (up to 5000 words)

To some students 5000 words does not seem a particularly long essay. They are the lucky few who find writing comes easily and who welcome the opportunity to produce a more detailed essay. To many students, however, 5000 words represents something of a mountain to climb. After all, what is it that takes so many words to say? How do you fill out an essay of this length and make it worthwhile? Can there really be 5000 words to describe a Shakespeare play or the Great Exhibition of 1851? Behind such questions is perhaps a sense that the longer the essay, the greater the risk of things going wrong. This is obviously true: the more you write, the more chance there is for the essay to wander off course or for your writing to become sloppy. It is also the case that many longer essays that start off well run out of steam at about the 2000-word point, that is, at the point where the student usually expects to end the essay. Sometimes this is because the student simply hasn't got enough primary material – he or she hasn't read the text or got involved with the topic being written about – but more often than not it is simply that the student cannot quite figure out how to produce a sustained piece of work.

By this stage it ought to come as no surprise that we are going to suggest that a three-step method can also be applied to longer essays. And, just as with the other writing assessments discussed so far, what can really help is having a specific number of paragraphs in mind so that you can sift and sort your ideas. Instead of a blank piece of paper or a torrent of notes, having a structure for your essay starts to organise your material in a much more substantial way but also identifies any gaps or shortcomings you might need to address. What we suggest is that you try to think, in fact, in terms of 20 paragraphs. As with shorter essays, in the opening state the topic and try to divide the subject into three. If, for example, the topic was the Great Exhibition, you might split it into a description, its contemporary effect and then, thirdly, its historical and cultural significance. But in addition to planning your essays in terms of the number of paragraphs, you might find it helpful, as with reports, to see the essay in terms of discrete sections:

1 paragraph (introduction)

6 paragraphs (section I)

6 paragraphs (section II)

6 paragraphs (section III)

1 paragraph (conclusion)

The logic of using sections is that, as with reports, it gives the essay a certain formality as well as a series of stopping points where you can take stock in a very measured way. Rather than simply calling the sections I, II and III, subheadings can be used as signposts to direct the reader and to alert your audience to a shift in the developing argument. For example, an essay on 'Keats and Language' might begin with the letters and their language, then move on to the longer poems and their vocabulary, and finally examine the Odes and their diction. The subheadings might be as plain as these, or phrased slightly more interestingly: 'Keats's letters and description', 'The language of narrative in the longer poems', 'The Odes, desire and language'. But make sure the subheadings are understandable; avoid questions and clever-clever titles. In addition to helping your reader, you may find that your subheadings also direct your own thinking and make it much more focused.

But what of the sections themselves? Is there a way of managing them? The answer is to think of plots within plots, that each section is a stage of the larger argument, but within each section you need to mount an argument that develops in a logical way from straightforward material through to more interesting ideas and a more complicated understanding of the issues. Think of each section as following the basic format of the essay we discussed in Unit 62: set it up/push it along/push your luck. There is a need, in other words, to make sure each stage of the essay earns its keep and does not simply fill in details. The essay has to explore and build as it goes along. It is no use relying on the first or the last few pages to do all the work. An essay that is interesting for just one or two pages will receive lower marks than an essay which, though not quite as original, nevertheless makes a sustained effort and arrives somewhere fresh on the basis of a well-wrought argument.

The real advantage of a longer essay is, of course, that it provides room for you to explore a topic in considerable depth, to show a range of reading and to demonstrate your skills. On the positive side, having a steady structure for the essay means that you concentrate precisely on the topic and on showing that you know how to manage a more sophisticated exercise than a brief essay. What is also involved, however, is that as you take on longer pieces of work you will come to see how the writing itself is part of the process of learning. Instead of essays acting as a sort of container of your ideas, you will come to appreciate more and more how writing an essay actually creates the knowledge that it is discussing: that the knowledge contained in an essay is not somehow separate from the language of the essay, but rather that the two are intrinsically linked. This is even more the case with a dissertation.

▶ 87 Dissertations (10,000/15,000/20,000 words)

To some extent the dissertation is just another piece of writing in which students can show what they know and what they have learned. Its main point is that it allows you to put forward a substantial argument or piece of individual research of up to, in some cases, 20,000 words. It might, for example, be on a particular theme such as 'The Politics of Home in Children's Literature', or on a particular historical event or dealing with a topic such as the ethics of cloning. One of the main attractions of the dissertation is the chance to set and develop your work as an independent learner outside the staid formula of set books and required essay topics. Without wanting to take away any of this freedom and inventiveness, we nevertheless want to suggest that a really good dissertation can also be achieved through thinking about its structure as much as its content.

Unlike other exercises, however, with a dissertation you are not normally given a title but have to make up your own title as well as choose the area you wish to write about or work on. This is one reason why the dissertation is often seen as more challenging and more demanding than other pieces of assessment and why, too, it is sometimes decisive in the final grading of students at university. More than with other exercises, it seems as if you are on your own. While your supervisor might prompt you about how to get started, and while your department may provide you with dissertation guidelines and even specimen examples, there is nevertheless a feeling about the exercise that it is a somehow more individual effort that will reveal the truth about you. This may be so, but what the dissertation or thesis really reveals is how well you can plan and execute an interesting piece of work.

And that is not difficult. If you have read this far in this book and not skipped too many units, you will already have an idea of how you might tackle your dissertation project. Even without a title or a clue about what you might choose to write about, you will know that it will help if you divide your material into three so that it has a clear, manageable structure. What we suggest is that you think in terms of three chapters (plus an introduction and perhaps a brief conclusion), with roughly 11 paragraphs per chapter: this will give you the equivalent of writing three essays of about 2500–3000 words. Each chapter, that is, can follow the format of the longer essay plan discussed above in Unit 84. For longer dissertations of, say, 20,000 words, you might think of three chapters with 20 paragraphs in each.

All of this might seem almost too pat. Can it really be the case that knowing how many paragraphs your dissertation will have can actually help? Surely there is more to it than this? The answer is 'yes and no'. Yes, because, quite obviously, to write at length about, say, *Hamlet* and death, you are going to have to read the play and think about it, especially if you want a new angle at some point. No, because knowing how your essay will pan out means you can fit everything into a preexisting format. More than this, though, knowing what the shape and structure of your dissertation is going to be will help you with the first stage of thinking about what area to work on and even how to formulate your title. Take our dissertation on *Hamlet* and death. As it stands, it is rather a bland title that gives the reader little clue as to what the dissertation might really be about. If, however, we think in terms of a structure of three sections or chapters, it seems clear that we would do better with a title that related to that structure: Death in *Hamlet*: Suicide, Murder and Revenge. Setting up your title in this way immediately gives the dissertation a shape and form that it lacked previously. In the end, the title might change from this as you discover more about the topic, but having this kind of clear starting point means you can begin planning your work in a more purposeful way and also start thinking through your ideas.

We have stressed this organisational planning of the dissertation because one of the characteristic weaknesses of dissertations is the lack of control not just over the argument but also over the choice of material. This starts with the topic itself: it is either too huge or too small. A dissertation on all of Dickens's novels is always going to have too much to cover; a dissertation on a single novel might work, but it will need supplementary material to sustain an argument, or a title such as that which we have devised for our *Hamlet* essay, with its three topics. By contrast, a dissertation on three Dickens novels organises itself almost without effort. Similarly, a dissertation about pollution, for example, that takes land, air and water as its subject areas has a logic to it, but it remains vast, whereas a project on three aspects of water pollution already has an internal coherence.

What, though, of the dissertation chapters themselves? What should you be working towards in these? We noted above how each chapter might follow the shape of the 11-paragraph essays described in Unit 84:

Chapter One

Introduction

Paragraphs 2, 3 and 4

Paragraphs 5, 6 and 7

Paragraphs 8, 9 and 10

Final rounding-off paragraph.

As with any essay, the object in each chapter is to build an argument in stages, going from a clear starting point and working towards a more complex, interesting conclusion. The danger, however, with the dissertation is that you might feel that there is, paradoxically, little room to be inventive or imaginative in your ideas, that what is required is more like a report than an essay. In some subjects, it is true that the dissertation contains a great deal of data or has to begin with a litera-ture survey and a review of the field. This is especially the case with the social sciences and science-style projects, but even here the actual quality of the analysis of the information matters a great deal. In other words, even in the most factual-based dissertation what the examiners are looking for, and will reward, is not just a regurgitation of the basics but evidence that you have thought about your topic in an intelligent way. There is, then, every reason to think of each chapter as an opportunity to explore the issues being discussed in a fresh way. This is the real secret of the dissertation. Superficially, it may look like an exercise in showing everything you have learned about a topic and demonstrating that you can handle large chunks of information, but what really brings a dissertation to life is all the little details you spot and how you present them in a logical, orderly way.

▶ 88 Salvage operations on essays, reports and dissertations

No matter how hard you try, sometimes an essay will not come together. Or you might have written your essay in draft, but then see that it is all over the place, leaping from idea to idea. Some pages may have ten paragraphs on them, others none at all. If your essay looks bitty, or looks crowded, the chances are that it is exactly that. But there is a way of salvaging essays like this, and that is to impose a shape on them. In the case of a shortish essay of 1500 words or so, it is fairly easy to impose a grid of 8 paragraphs and turn the essay into a more coherent, sensible shape. Similarly, with longer essays you can use 11 paragraphs, or 20 paragraphs for 5000-word essays. Or, with a dissertation, divide it into three chapters and it will immediately start to take on a new aspect.

Of course, just linking up sentences into paragraphs won't solve all the problems of a very bitty piece of work. You will need here and there to ease the sentences into one another by linking them so that the reader isn't suddenly jolted from one point to the next. Or you may have to cut a sentence that simply repeats a point. But once you do start organising your work through imposing a shape on it, it will quickly start to become ordered and cohesive. Indeed, if you have been following the logic of this book, you may well find that you have almost automatically been organising your work in blocks so that what appears a ragbag collection of sentences simply needs a little bit of editing, for example, in the kind of way described earlier when we looked at university application forms. Tighten your sentences up so that they relate to one another and the paragraph will soon become well defined.

An example. This is the opening of the poor science essay we looked at in Section 8 (Unit 73):

> A scientific method has been used since science began. It has played an extremely important role in the understanding of the Earth and the many things that occur within, on, and around it.
>
> In this essay I am going to discuss the scientific method by which data is analysed to produce a theory or to test a hypothesis in the Earth Sciences. The method will then be looked at in the other disciplines and similarities and differences will be discussed.
>
> The method consists of a number of steps that can be varied depending on the accuracy of the experiment to which it is applied. These include both practical and mental applications that hopefully produce a precise and relevant outcome when completed.
>
> This outcome can then be analysed further and applied in similar situations to that in which it was first found.

This looks disjointed and reads awkwardly. Here is the same opening with a bit of tinkering:

> In this essay I am going to discuss the scientific method by which data is analysed to produce a theory or to test a hypothesis in the Earth Sciences. The method consists of a number of steps that can be varied depending on the accuracy of the experiment to which it is applied. These include both practical and mental applications that hopefully produce a precise and relevant outcome when completed. This outcome can then be analysed further and applied in similar situations to that in which it was first found.

All that has happened here is that the original bitty paragraphs have been brought together as one unit and any repetition and dead wood cut out. Now each sentence connects with the one before to form a coherent sequence. Paragraph discipline of this kind can rescue almost any piece of writing, however bad the situation looks. By the same token, a whole rough draft of a dissertation can be brought into shape by using the same methods. Start by identifying the larger units or sections, numbering them or giving them titles if chapters. Then look at the organisation of each chapter or section: does it have a paragraph logic, moving from setting up the topic through to a more complex understanding of the material? And what of each paragraph? Does it have a beginning, middle and end? In some cases you may need to move a paragraph, but most often you will find that you need to add a few phrases to link paragraphs so that the argument flows.

The trick with all salvage operations, then, is to see that every essay is rescuable; every essay has the potential to become an effective piece of writing. First, identify the problem: is it a long, sprawling essay or a bitty, messy piece that lacks a clear thread of argument? In both cases the answer is to impose a more regular shape on the essay, trimming long paragraphs or knitting up straggling ones. Secondly, check that the introduction doesn't overreach itself, making so many points that the rest of the essay has nowhere to go. Finally, look at the beginning and end of each paragraph: does it pick up the argument from the previous paragraph and end by drawing the argument together? Once you have done this, the essay should be ready for its final check-over, the subject of the next unit.

▶ 89 The importance of editing and polishing

Having written your essay, the natural response is to breathe a sigh of relief and to hand it in as soon as possible, hoping it will get a good mark. But most students who get good marks know that merely writing the essay is only the first stage and that a good essay will require some additional work – but not much. The good news is that once you have completed a draft of your essay you have done most of the hard slog. The other things you have to do to an essay are less laborious but can also make a significant difference. And they are fairly easy to do. They involve editing the essay for mistakes and errors, and, secondly, polishing the essay to improve it.

The first thing to do, however, is to put the essay away for a day or so. In other words, once you have written your essay, put it aside for a while so that you can come back to it fresh. In order to check your essay you need to be able to stand back from it and see it as a piece of writing. This means being able to see both its form and its content. Start with, and check, the simple things first: have you got the title down correctly? You would be surprised how many essays are submitted with spelling mistakes in the title. And then check that all your sentences have full stops. Do all your sentences make sense? Are there any spelling errors or punctuation errors or words omitted from them? Editing is very often a matter of spotting small errors that undermine the quality of an essay and suggest a degree of carelessness on the part of the writer. On the other hand, an essay with very few errors immediately gives an impression of competence and professionalism.

As well as checking mechanical aspects of the essay – spelling, punctuation, and grammar – check that the quotations are accurate and that the notes and any bibliography are correct. It is all too easy at the end of drafting an essay to make slips or get details wrong. Remember, the reader is interested in how you have performed the task as a whole, not just in the first few pages of the essay. An accumulation of small mistakes may lead the marker to feel that he or she can't really trust the quality of your argument, that if you get small things wrong you are likely to get everything else wrong as well. It's just like leaving the hand-brake on during the driving test: it doesn't stop the car from moving but it suggests a lack of skill and knowledge on the part of the learner.

If editing is about the mechanical aspects of an essay and making sure you get things right, polishing looks to ways of improving the real substance of the essay. Here three simple tips can suffice. First, make sure you don't endlessly repeat a word or phrase. Overused words lose their force, so replacing them adds variety and strength to your writing. Similarly, check that you don't begin sentences in the same way. It is very easy to slip into a whole series of sentences beginning 'It is' or 'This shows' or, worse, 'Therefore' or 'So'. Such sentences can often be rewritten by a slight change of word order or phrase. Finally, check how your essay ends. A good ending can reinforce the strengths of the essay. A short, final sentence can give an essay a lift: it is as if you have thought through your argument and can really see for yourself where it has arrived. But if you can't think of a short sentence, don't invent one just to conform to our advice. And try to avoid ending with a quotation from a critic or a book, since that gives someone else the last word. If you use a quotation, add a few words of your own as the final essay comment.

This rule about how to use secondary sources applies to your essay as whole. Students sometimes feel that they have to quote from other people and that other people's words make the point much better than they could. Indeed, sometimes students submit essays that are really a kind of patchwork of views drawn from books or articles, with the student adding little more than 'This is supported by Professor Smart', or 'In the words of Ewan Mee'. If you find you have written an essay like this, then you will need to undertake some further work on it. Many of the points made by other people can be put in your own words or summarised very easily. More often than not they are drawing attention to details that you have also spotted, but not quite had the time to think about how to phrase. Usually you will find that perhaps only one of them is really saying anything special that you need for your argument.

There is, though, another particularly important reason for examining your use of secondary sources. This is plagiarism. 'Plagiarism' means using or borrowing other people's ideas or words without properly acknowledging them in your essay and notes. In simple terms, it is cheating. The crude form of plagiarism involves copying out chunks of a book or article or picking out sentences from different parts of someone else's work and patching them together. Both of these forms are easy to spot and you will receive a mark of zero for the essay. Sometimes, however, students accidentally plagiarise: they read a sentence or a phrase and think it will sit nicely in their essay, giving it a bit more style or substance. What they forget is that such borrowings will stick out like a sore thumb: they will read and sound differently from the rest of the essay. Remember, in these days of sophisticated computer technology it is very easy to trace unacknowledged borrowings; search engines and plagiarism software mean that suspect work can be checked in seconds.

There is, however, no real need for plagiarism. It is, in fact, relatively easy to turn an essay built around quotations into a more independent piece of writing. Certainly you must make it clear whenever you are drawing on another person's work or words, but, as suggested above, you can then suggest that the person cited has not quite got the full measure of the problem, or you can disagree with their view. Of course, this can be difficult in science subjects or law, where so much depends on previous knowledge, but even here it is possible to present the quotation in such a way as to leave you free to move forward with your own additional or related ideas. This may take more time to learn as a skill than in the humanities, where it is almost a norm to disagree or modify other authors' views, but the skill can be learnt by the use of careful phrasing at the polishing stage. Adding a few words – 'This is perhaps best summed up'; 'This has been well put if somewhat awkwardly by' – can suggest that you really are in charge of the essay in the same way that your careful ordering of your paragraphs does.

Editing and polishing, then, involves checking and correcting errors, and also making sure that the essay reflects your own work and ideas. But it also involves adding a touch of refinement to your writing. Judging your own work and paying attention to what you write and how you write is probably the most important skill to learn, but the advantages it brings are enormous.

▶ 90 Examinations

Most students prepare well and sensibly for exams. They work through their notes, reading them over and often making summaries of key points and details. In addition, many students use highlighter pens to mark up what they regard as the central information to be learnt or used in the exam in a very direct way. In science subjects, for example, one might be asked to describe a certain feature or experiment or to answer a number of short, factual questions. In humanities subjects, students are expected to be familiar with a range of material and to have read the basic texts. There are no shortcuts around these preparation processes. No essay method can save you from doing the initial work for your course or from preparing for the examinations. Sometimes, however, students over-prepare the content of their exam answers at the expense of thinking about the shape and form of their answer. They may have learnt all there is to know about a subject, but have no strategy for answering the questions.

A simple example will help to explain the point we are making. You are a first-year university student taking a module on poetry. You are reasonably certain that there is going to be a question on the sonnet, although its exact wording is, of course, not yet known. You know that you are expected to demonstrate a range of reading in your answer and to show that you have thought about the sonnet as a specific kind of poem. As part of your preparation you read a number of sonnets from different periods and by different authors. All seems well in terms of basic preparation: you know the main points about the various forms of sonnet and the various ways in which it has been used in relation to various themes. In the exam you write all of this down, but are disappointed that your mark for the module is just average. Somehow all the effort of preparation and revision has failed to pay off.

There could, of course, be many reasons why an exam answer doesn't quite receive the mark you expected, but one particular reason might be the way in which the answer is planned and delivered. There are various methods of planning an examination answer that students employ, including the web method where a whole series of points is attached to threads from a central point to form a sort of spider's web. To our mind, that is an approach that wastes far too much time in the exam room as students first write down as many points as they can remember and then try to convert it all into an essay. The method we recommend, predictably enough, is to think in terms of three stages and divide your material accordingly. Even if the method is developed no further than this, having a predetermined structure for your answer will lend it an important feature: it will have the shape of an argument, rather than being merely a list of points or examples.

If we go back to our sonnet question, there is an obvious danger that the answer will turn into a rather flat description of the different kinds of sonnet by different poets, with no real sense of a problem being discussed and analysed. The same is true with almost any answer where the question seems just to want an account of something and where, initially, there seems to be little sense of a problem or issue: a sonnet is a sonnet, it has fourteen lines and lots of poets write them. What could be simpler? But clearly, if this is all there were to the answer, the question would not be set. There must be more to the matter, and it is up to you in your answer to suggest as much.

The simplest way of doing this is to return to the basic essay method we described earlier in this book and to see your answer in three stages. In the first stage you set your answer up, dealing with the most obvious aspect of the topic: that sonnets have a recognisable form and pattern but a number of rhyme schemes. In the second stage you deal with the second aspect and push the essay along: that despite appearing to be a set form, the sonnet seems able to sustain a variety of topics. Finally, in the third stage you deal with the more complex aspect of the topic, pushing your luck by extending your argument and ideas: that the sonnet seems the most paradoxical of forms by being at once the most restricted yet most open of poetic kinds. Almost every answer can follow this simple shape in which you first introduce the topic, then push on with the straightforward material, and then, in the final third, move on to the contradictions or complications inherent in the topic.

We ought to be clear here, however. We have suggested that every question sets a problem and that in your answer you should seek to draw this out, that as you build your answer you develop a case that highlights the complexity of the issue addressed in the question set. We are not suggesting, of course, that in your answer you invent difficulties or dream up problems – that sonnets, for example, would be better if they were longer, or shorter; that the First World War had no causes; or that pollution could be ended if trees ruled the world. This is not what we mean. Rather, what we are referring to is the way in which you can show that you have thought through the topic you are dealing with, and how you can see that it amounts to something more than just a straightforward matter. In effect, you are saying that you can see through to the real issues the question raises.

There is, as you might expect, an additional benefit to thinking of your answer in terms of a three-stage argument, and that has to do with your exam preparation. If you have a clear idea of the kind of essay you may be writing, and the kind of stages your argument will be following, then it is possible to use that structure to organise your exam preparation. As you read through your material it makes sense to think about where you will deploy it: is it fairly straightforward material that you would be expected to know, or is it more complex material that might best be used towards the end of the essay? Have you got too much basic material that illustrates the same point and will simply fill out the answer, but nothing for the later stages of your discussion where you want to highlight the complexity of the issues raised? Working through your notes with these questions in mind will also help arrange them in a more subtle order than just a series of points. The strategy, as ever, is to make the most of your hard work, but also to let your essay structure do some of that work for you.

10 Taking Stock

▶ **91 Writers on writing**

A lot of people who drive become tremendously interested in cars, buying car magazines, watching motoring programmes on televison, and knowing all manner of things far in excess of what they actually need to know to get from one place to another. Obviously, people get interested in football, fishing, music, celebrities and a host of other subjects in a similar kind of way; they become self-appointed experts in their own fields of interest. If you think about it, you are going to spend a lot of your working life writing. If you teach, work in an office, work in industry or in the service or retail sector, you are nearly always going to have a pen in your hand or be working at a computer screen. And when you aren't writing, you'll be talking; there really is no escape from working with words.

It follows, therefore, that you might think about developing the kind of interest in words and writing that we take for granted in relation to hobbies such as cars, football and fishing. It is a vast subject; there is so much to learn, so much to know, and so much of it is fascinating. It is the fascination of words that we try to convey in this final section. Much of what we have included might seem trivial, but this is never entirely the case. An awareness of such matters makes us sensitive to writing as an activity; it helps move us beyond an automatic, almost casual use of words. We become aware of the craft of writing and the power of words. And when we write, the possibility is that we might write with an extra degree of alertness to wanting to make language work for us.

This should start to become apparent if we look at some of the things that writers have said about writing. We have taken the comments from a selection in *The Penguin Dictionary of Modern Humorous Quotations*, compiled by Fred Medcalf; all writers like to build up a bookshelf of useful books, and this is one of the staple books that every budding writer would probably want to own. The point that is reiterated more than any other when writers comment on writing is that good writing takes time. As we have suggested throughout this book, a first draft is just that, a first draft; there is still a lot of polishing and redrafting that has to be done before you arrive at something you feel happy with. Some people take this to an extreme. In the words of Oscar Wilde: 'I was working on the proof of one of my poems all the morning, and took out a comma. In the afternoon I put it back again.' Vladimir Nabokov is equally aware of the importance of polishing and revision: 'Only ambitious nonentities and hearty mediocrities exhibit their rough drafts. It's like passing round samples of one's sputum.' And as Lillian Hellman says: 'Nothing you write, if you hope to be any good, will ever come out as you first hoped.' Remember, therefore, along with Isaac Bashevis Singer, that a 'waste paper basket is the writer's best friend'.

If you hate the moment when you actually have to start writing, you are not alone. Peter de Vries says it all: 'I love being a writer. What I can't stand is the paperwork.' And Fran Lebowitz expands the point very effectively: 'Contrary to what many of you might imagine, a career in letters is not without its drawbacks – chief among them the unpleasant fact that one is frequently called upon to sit down and write.' Most of us have probably felt as desperate as Gene Fowler: 'Writing is easy; all you do is sit staring at a blank sheet of paper until the drops of blood form on your forehead.' But we have to sit down and force ourselves to write. And there is light at the end of the tunnel. Along with Michael Kanin, we can appreciate the afterglow of: 'I don't like to write, but I love to have written.'

More specifically on how to write, Ezra Pound and Evelyn Waugh have relevant things to say about two of the central points we have stressed in this book. One is that you are writing for an audience, and you have to hold the reader's attention at all times. Pound puts it rather cynically: 'The secret of popular writing is never to put more on a given page than the common reader can lap off it with no strain whatsoever on his habitually slack attention.' You might feel that this does not apply to the essays you are writing as a student, but the fact is that the person reading the essay wants you to do all the work. They don't want to be in the position of trying to work out what you are getting at; they want you to hold their hand and lead them through the subject. And one of the secrets of this is writing in plain and straightforward English. This is Evelyn Waugh in his 1938 novel *Scoop*, the kind of novel that people interested in writing are likely to want to read:

> 'He's supposed to have a particularly high-class style: "Feather-footed through the splashy fen passes the questing vole" . . . would that be it?'
>
> 'Yes,' said the Managing Editor. 'That must be good style. At least it doesn't sound like anything else to me.'

When you write, you shouldn't be aiming to write something that doesn't sound like anything else; you should be aiming to say what you have to say in the clearest and most readable way.

And even when you have finished, someone else will always have a view about how it can be improved. H. G. Wells writes: 'No passion in the world is equal to the passion to alter someone else's draft.' As a writer – and, as someone at school, college or university writing an essay, you are just as much a writer as William Shakespeare, Jane Austen or Charles Dickens – you should feel compelled to keep on tinkering, polishing and perfecting every sentence you have written.

▶ 92 When in doubt, strike it out

'You need to go away and polish this. It really needs another draft.' Students often receive such advice; normally, however, they aren't told how to redraft. We hope we have explained how to do it during the course of this book, but we want to repeat one of the most important points. It's nearly always possible to say what you want to say in fewer words, and it will probably be said more effectively if you say it in fewer words. Indeed, what often matters most about an essay is what is cut out so that what remains is relevant and sharply focused.

Alexander Pope writes: 'Words are like leaves; and where they most abound, Much fruit of sense is rarely found.' But we prefer Anatole France, because he says much the same thing in fewer words: 'The best sentence? The shortest.' We can become more precise, however, if we pay attention to Mark Twain: 'As to the adjective, when in doubt, strike it out.' Adjectives are those words that describe nouns, as in 'perfect day' or 'dark night'. It is often said that adjectives are frail, and we should not ask them to do more work than they should. The real danger is in descriptive writing, where there is a great temptation (which could probably be abbreviated to temptation – the adjective 'great' didn't really add anything) to accumulate adjectives: 'The swirling, dark, dangerous, soul-destroying, angry sea.' As is so often the case, writing to make an impression can provoke the reader to a feeling of depression. Far from being an act of inspired genius, there is something lazy about writing down every word that comes to mind when one, or even none, would do. We feel that the three words 'The angry sea' convey rather more than the eight words originally used.

Another area where the delete button on the computer could profitably be employed is in connection with the 'pride and prejudice problem'. Students feel that if they write a sentence where they double up the adjectives with a linking 'and' this will add some extra authority to their work. They might write, for example, about the 'social and cultural history of the nineteenth century'. But it would be better to choose just one of the adjectives; the choice of two words is usually just a rhetorical flourish, adding nothing to the real meaning. In most circumstances even more words can get lost. Why not just write, 'In the nineteenth century'? We have called this the 'pride and prejudice problem' because *Pride and Prejudice* is the title of a Jane Austen novel, and it is a construction that she uses all the time in her works. It is integral to the meaning of her novels, because it enables her to privilege an idea of balance, a social concept that she is keen to endorse. And Jane Austen uses the technique brilliantly. But in most student essays there is more than a hint of redundancy in the unnecessary proliferation of balancing terms. Part of the valuable process of redrafting is to decide which adjective, if any, does the required job in an essay.

▶ 93 Is making a fuss about splitting infinitives just splitting hairs?

'To never split an infinitive is quite easy.' Before moving on, do you know why pedants would disapprove of that sentence? By the infinitive we mean the 'to' form of the verb: 'to go', 'to see', 'to love'. These are all infinitive forms. An infinitive is split when a word (usually an adverb) is inserted between the 'to' and the base form of the verb: 'to boldly go', 'to quickly see', 'to passionately love'. Traditionalists argue that (because Latin verbs cannot be split) such splitting is ungrammatical and should be avoided; other people argue it should be avoided on stylistic grounds as inelegant. Most people, of course, cannot tell the difference between a split infinitive and a banana split. And that is exactly as it should be. It doesn't matter if people split infinitives when writing.

But a person who is interested in writing – and the person who is interested in writing is someone who, every day, is becoming a better writer – should at least be able to recognise a split infinitive. It is part of the process of standing back critically from the words one has written, or the words someone else has written, and looking at the medium in which the ideas have been conveyed. Most of us would be able to tell instantly if someone was wearing a tie that clashed hideously with their shirt. And most of us would reckon that we could judge when people had made less extreme, but slightly jarring, blunders with their clothes. As a writer, you should be looking at language in the same way, becoming sensitive to small lapses of taste.

There are times when it is necessary to split an infinitive to clarify meaning. For example, if we wrote 'He failed to entirely comprehend me,' it might be a split infinitive, but the correct version is not an improvement: 'He failed to comprehend me entirely.' This second version could possibly mean that the person failed to understand anything about me, whereas the intended meaning is that the person didn't grasp the full sense of what was being said; the reason for splitting the infinitive is to bring the adverb next to the verb it modifies. But the person who was serious about polishing their work would probably realise that there is something a touch inflated about what had originally been written, and look for shorter, easier words and a simpler way of saying it: 'He did not understand everything I had said.' This is part of the general logic of writing: that there is nearly always another, usually simpler and better, way of writing anything. Sometimes, however, a split infinitive is the only choice. Nobody would want to sacrifice the famous words from *Star Trek*: 'To boldly go where no man has gone before.' If, as in this case, it is a famous quotation, it isn't your job to correct the use of English.

▶ 94 An alphabet of errors

The split infinitive is just one of those small details in writing that it is so easy to get wrong. All of us make mistakes from time to time. In every essay, even by the most able students, there will always be the odd misplaced comma or the occasional spelling mistake. And there are always at least a couple of errors in every book ever published. Mistakes are unavoidable. But try to avoid silly mistakes that stem from not thinking carefully about your work. Over the course of the next few pages we run through a list of some of the most common errors (some of these rules do not apply in the USA).

Accommodation   It is said that a certain university used to invite students for an Open Day, asking them if they required overnight accommodation. Those who wrote back spelling the word accommodation correctly were offered a place; those who spelt it incorrectly were rejected. The correct spelling is 'accommodation'; the way that people always spell it incorrectly is '*accomodation'. It might help if you remember that accommodation has double cc and double mm: two up and two down, as it were.

All right   Never write '*alright'. The TV programme should be called *It'll Be All Right on the Night*. What they call it is *It'll Be Alright on the Night*, and that's poor English.

Argument   No *e* after *u* – and you can't argue with that.

Breach   'Breach', with an *a*, means 'breaking a rule or agreement'. 'Breech' means the rear part of the body (as in 'breech birth') or the part of a gun behind the barrel.

Continuous   'Continuous' and 'continual' are often confused. 'Continuous' means 'without interruption'. 'Continual' admits a break. Noisy neighbours might be a continual nuisance, but would only be a continuous nuisance if they made a noise 24 hours a day every day.

Definite   No *a* in this word, despite the attempts of millions to insert one. It's 'definite', not '*definate'. And it's definitely not '*definately'.

Effect and affect   'Affect' means 'to have an influence on'. 'Effect' means 'to accomplish'. A politician, for example, can affect many people, but might not realise just what an effect he has had on their lives.

Flaunt and flout   'Flaunt' means 'to show off', whereas 'flout' means 'to defy convention'.

Fulfil   Has just one *l* at the end.

Gorilla   The animal is a 'gorilla'. 'Guerrilla warfare' is something quite different, deriving from the Spanish word for war, *guerra*. The spellings 'guerilla' and 'guerrilla' are both acceptable, but 'guerrilla' is preferred.

Hello, hallo, hullo   Each of these spellings is acceptable, but 'hello' is used most commonly.

Imply   Students often use the words 'imply' and 'infer' in essays, and often use the wrong word. 'Imply' means 'to suggest or hint at'; 'infer' means 'to deduce or conclude' something.

Judgement   The spelling 'judgment' is equally acceptable, and preferred in a legal context.

Kilometre   It is important to realise that some words like this end with *re* and some with *er*. Distances end *re*, because we are using a French word, but we measure things with a 'meter'. In relation to poetry, we talk about the 'metre' of a poem, but in compounds referring to the number of measures in a line this, confusingly, reverts to an *er* ending, as in 'pentameter'.

Learned   'Learned' and 'learnt' are equally acceptable.

Millennium   Note the second *n*. At the time of the Millennium cele-brations, about 20 per cent of the time it was incorrectly spelt as '*millenium'.

Not only   If you write 'Not only', you must balance the clause with 'but also'. You can't write, '*I have lost not only my job but my good name.' You have to write, 'I have lost not only my job but also my good name.'

Occurrence   There are words that are notoriously difficult to spell correctly. This is one of them. If you are typing an essay, you must always use the Spellcheck. If you are writing an answer in an exam-ination, if there is a word you are unsure how to spell there is nearly always going to be a shorter, easier and probably better word that can be substituted.

Parallel   Two *a*'s, two *ll*'s and then *el*.

Psychology   *P* before *s*.

Queueing   Sometimes when *ing* is added the final *e* disappears from the original (as in 'breathe' and 'breathing'). It is, in fact, quite acceptable to use 'queuing' rather than 'queueing', but there are lots of words where there isn't the same luxury of choice. If you are at all in doubt, you must make a point of checking *ing* endings, and also *able* and *ible* endings.

Rhythm   This is a tricky word to spell, probably because it sounds as if it has a vowel in it, but it doesn't (although *y* is functioning as a vowel).

Separate   Has two *e*'s separated by two *a*'s.

Thank you   Two words. Don't write '*thankyou'.

Tragedy   This is the correct way to spell it. Students often add an extra *d* before the *g*: '*tradgedy'.

Until   Has one *l*.

Venue   The original guide to effective writing was Fowler's *Modern English Usage*, first published in 1926. One of the many good points made by Fowler is that 'venue' is an affected and unnecessary word. What people mean is 'place'. What Fowler said in 1926 is still just as true today; there is nearly always a simpler word that can be substi-tuted for a pretentious word. The simple word, paradoxically, makes what someone has written sound more grown-up.

While   On the same subject as the previous entry, why would anyone write 'whilst' when what they mean is 'while'. 'Whilst' is a ridiculous affectation that tries to give writing a more literary air. 'Whilst' is just the kind of word you should be pruning from your essays as you go through them polishing and tightening what you have written.

X-ray   This is an unusual word in that, although it has been around for years, the hyphen is retained. Generally, as in 'email', the hyphen disappears as the word becomes more and more used. The other unusual thing about 'X-ray' is that it is normally used with a capital letter at the start: 'I've got to have an X-ray.' But it is quite all right to use lower case with the verb. One could, therefore, write either 'I've just been X-rayed' or 'I've just been x-rayed.'

Your   'Your' means 'belonging to you'. Make sure that is what you mean. If you write 'you're' that is an abbreviation of 'you are'. Note also the spelling 'yours'; don't be tempted to write '*your's'.

Zzz   We imagine that anyone who has persevered with reading the list above has probably dropped off to sleep by now. Nobody expects you to know all the little rules about spelling and usage. It is, of course, the case that the more that you write the more you will become aware of them. And they are things that one should be thinking about when writing, and particularly when checking work. Where, for example, two spellings of a word are acceptable, only one of them should be used in a piece of writing, rather than alternating between them. If there is anything you are unsure about, your first resource is the Internet. Type the word or words you are unsure about into Google, and perhaps other words like 'how to spell' or 'meaning of', and you will discover that there are hundreds of websites that discuss and explain every aspect of language. But there are also books that you can buy. Most people own a dictionary, but it's also nice to own books about words and language. Again, use the Internet to find these books. If you look up this book on the Amazon website, for example, reference will be made to other books that cover the same broad field. Most students are quite happy to buy the textbooks for their subject, but as you are going to spend so much of your time as a student writing you should also consider building up a collection of books about writing.

▶ 95 Why is English so awkward?

If we talk about 'a little old man', native speakers of English know that this is the correct sequence. We wouldn't feel comfortable with 'an old little man'. The instinct would be to slip in a comma – 'an old, little man' – as the idea seems to be different from what is suggested in the 'natural' order of 'a little old man'. There are rules that govern the sequence. We move through what is observed, as in this man's size, then the physical description – in which the sequence is generally size, shape, age, colour – then origin and finally material. For example, we might conceivably see 'a beautiful, small, round, old, red, Italian, wooden ornament'. It's not a very realistic proposition, but the fact is that most of us have internalised, without ever consciously learning, the rules that govern such things as sequence. Think how difficult it must be for someone learning English who just cannot grasp the intricacies of spoken English. A lot of other languages are far more logical, or appear so because they have many more visible grammatical features.

One of the reasons English is so rich, however, is because it is a hybrid language that has absorbed words, conventions, and good and bad habits from just about everywhere. It has a very varied vocabulary, enabling us to describe events and features in different ways. The story starts with invasions and three Germanic dialects – Jutish, Saxon and Anglian – which replaced the indigenous Celtic tongue. Subsequent Norse and Danish invasions left their mark, but the biggest impact came with the Norman invasion of 1066. English as we know it today very slowly began to evolve in the fourteenth century. But this is not the place to present a history of the English language. Those who are interested will almost certainly want to look at David Crystal's *Cambridge Encyclopedia of the English Language*, or Melvyn Bragg's *The Adventure of English*.

What we do want to note briefly, however, is how loan words have come into English. From China, words such as silk, typhoon, tea, tycoon. From Africa: banana, cola, tango. From Central America: avocado, chocolate, tomato. From the Caribbean: canoe, hammock, hurricane, maize, potato, tobacco, barbecue. From Malaysia: bamboo, sago, amok, compound, caddy, ketchup, sarong. From Tibet: polo, yak. From India: bungalow, cot, dungarees, juggernaut, bandana, jungle, shampoo, bangle, chutney, dinghy, gymkhana, loot, thug. From the Arab world: mattress, algebra, cotton, syrup, alcohol, arsenal, assassin, magazine, sash, tariff, alcove, sofa, zero, ghoul. The list could go on and on. It's little wonder that English, especially English spelling, is so unsystematic. What is also important to realise, however, is that it is the diversity of English that also makes it such a powerful language – not just powerful in the sense that it is spoken in the USA and, therefore, dominates as a kind of world language, but powerful in the sense that it is a language with an enormous vocabulary, and immense subtleties of tone and texture. The strength of the tradition of English literary culture has a lot to do with the strength of the language.

▶ 96 The importance of good manners

We live in a multi-cultural society. In whatever you write, therefore, you need to be alert to the way in which language can easily offend people, sometimes because of thoughtlessness on the part of the writer rather than any malicious intent. Try to be sure, for example, that your terminology is accurate and up to date when describing countries or peoples. Avoid stereotypes of race as well as of gender. Do not assume, in letters, that your addressee is male. Above all, be aware of the simple error of using 'he' as the norm of your writing. That problem disappears if you think of your readers rather than your reader and are aware that you are always addressing a variety of people with a variety of views

▶ 97 The importance of the right tone

'Don't talk to me in that tone of voice.' We all know what this sentence means. The speaker is upset or angry at the way something has been said: perhaps it was said with a snarl, or expressed an attitude of contempt. Whatever the problem, the speaker was not pleased with what they heard. When applied to writing, tone refers to the manner of writing, the combination of grammar, vocabulary and, to a lesser extent, the sound qualities of the language. In earlier units we have talked about avoiding slang and colloquialism. 'Hamlet is a well cool guy who thinks a lot' may be fine for a seminar joke, but trivialises Shakespeare's play when it occurs in an essay because it suggests a lack of effort and a lack of thought on the part of the writer.

But is it possible to be more precise about tone? How do you know if you are hitting the right writing note? One way is to steer clear of excess in any direction. Too much jargon can sound harsh and unapproachable. Long sentences full of polysyllables can strain the reader's attention; the reader stops listening to what you have to say. An official style, such as that used by bureaucrats, can dull the reader's eyes: 'The committee is concerned to ascertain sufficient information to satisfy itself and to expedite business in an appropriate manner so as to meet the challenges occasioned by the recent implementation of the new review methodology.' Just as troublesome is the over-writing associated with creativity, where every noun is accompanied by two adjectives, every verb by two adverbs and where images flitter across the page like butterflies on summer flowers or young birds in trees.

From all of this it might seem as if the best style is no style, or at least a very neutral style with a bland tone. We can put this more positively by saying that perhaps the best style, and therefore the best tone, is a grown-up style. That might sound a little dull, but it need not be. As with the essay structure itself, your writing can start off measured and formal, but as the essay begins to gather pace, your ideas and language can shift gear. By the end of an essay, you might find you can afford to introduce more theoretical points and more abstract vocabulary. What you need to avoid at all costs is writing in the language of pop culture. Britney Spears might include the words 'like' and 'awesome' in every sentence, but it is not appropriate in academic or formal writing. If you want to be taken seriously, you need to write in an appropriate voice and style.

▶ 98 An alphabet of advice

Apostrophes   If spelling was invented to make us all look foolish, the apostrophe was designed to drive teachers insane. The attempt to found a society dedicated to protecting the apostrophe seems only to have resulted in the proliferation of its misuse. Its real uses are very limited, and really quite easy to grasp:

1. To show possession in a noun: 'the dog's collar'
    *   The apostrophe precedes the *s* when the noun is singular: 'the girl's book', OR when the plural noun does not end in *s*: 'the men's jobs'.
    *   The apostrophe follows the *s* when the plural of the noun ends in *s*: 'the girls' books'.

2. To indicate that letters have been omitted:
    let's = let us; they're = they are; can't = cannot; it's = it is
    it's = it has ('it's gone wrong'); isn't = is not; who's = who is

    These contractions are all best avoided in formal essay writing. We have used them in this book in order to give the book a more informal, colloquial tone, but we would not use them in other contexts.

3. To show duration of time: 'two weeks' holiday', 'two hours' time'.

The following are always wrong:

'*potato's' instead of 'potatoes'
'*Keat's poetry' instead of 'Keats's poetry'
'*theirs'' instead of 'theirs' ('theirs is the car over there')

The apostrophe is now such a regular part of amusing errors in everyday life that it would be sad to see it disappear into too much correctness, especially at the greengrocer's.

Brackets Round brackets, also known as 'parentheses', enclose supplementary material that appears in a sentence, in a sense interrupting it. Use brackets sparingly. Think about our general instruction about losing words. Do you really need the extra bit in brackets? Only include it if you really do need it. Square brackets are used for brackets within brackets, and for editorial additions or amendments to a text that is being quoted. For example, 'The man [Tom] that Alice married'.

Capital letters For the most part capital letters cause few problems since they are used less and less outside the obvious places where they are needed:

People's names: Marilyn Monroe; W. B. Yeats
Words derived from proper names: 'Thatcherite'
Titles before names: Queen Elizabeth
Religious titles: the Holy Spirit
Names of countries, languages, towns, specific places, periods (the Renaissance)
Titles of books and organisations.

But we no longer use capitals for titles such as prime minister or president, unless they precede a person's name: President Chirac.

Disinterested 'Disinterested' does not mean 'uninterested'. You might be uninterested in football (that is, have no interest in it), but could be a Welshman who was a disinterested (that is, impartial or unconcerned) spectator at an England versus Scotland match. You might be really interested in the match, but probably would not be favouring either side.

Ellipses Ellipses are the three full stops that sometimes appear in the middle of quotations if words have been omitted: 'A man who knows [. . .] the value of nothing.' This is from Oscar Wilde's play *Lady Windermere's Fan*. The original is 'A man who knows the price of everything and the value of nothing.' We have put the ellipses in square brackets in order to indicate that they are editorial changes. This is because you will come across some texts where speeches break off in the middle of a sentence and this is indicated by ellipses. The square brackets show that the text has been changed by you rather than by the original author. In general, there is no need to insert ellipses at the beginning and end of quotations.

Fewer, less   'Fewer' is the comparative of 'few' and means 'not so many'. 'Less' is the comparative of 'little' and means 'not so much'. The difference between the two words might seem a fussy point, but when we are talking about countable things we generally use the adjective 'fewer', whereas when it is a measurable quantity that we cannot count we use 'less'. We might, for example, talk about having 'less energy'. But, as an additional complication, we use 'less' when a number is involved if the items are not being counted separately: 'I've less than forty pounds left in my account.' This is because the number here denotes an amount rather than a number of individual pounds. So, 'I've got fewer than six marbles left' is also correct.

Gerund   For some reason, everything people dread about grammar seems to be summed up in the word 'gerund'. The impression people have is that grammar amounts to difficult words to describe difficult concepts. We aren't going to say what a gerund is; if you are interested, there are plenty of grammar sites on the Internet. The reason we aren't defining it is to underline the point that we only need to know as much about grammar as enables us to become proficient writers. This present book contains all the technical information that any competent writer might require.

Hyphens   Hyphens are used to join two words together when they act as adjectives – for example, in the words 'nineteenth-century poetry', 'nineteenth-century' (adjective) describes the 'poetry' (noun) written in that period. But if we are talking about the 'nineteenth' (adjective) 'century' (noun), then there is no hyphen. There are other uses of the hyphen as well. In fractions ('two-thirds'), in words that begin with a prefix such as *ex* ('ex-husband'). But some words lose their hyphen very quickly through usage: 'e-mail' has become 'email' in general usage while we have been writing this book. We also use hyphens in writing out numbers between 21 and 99 – 'twenty-two', for example – as well as in compound nouns such as 'do-gooder', and other compounds before nouns: 'finger-lickin' chicken'.

Italics   Joseph Conrad's short novel *Heart of Darkness* begins, 'The *Nellie*, a cruising yawl . . . '. *The Nellie* is a ship, and italics are always used for the names of ships, aircraft and spacecraft. If you are using a word-processor, you can, as an alternative to italics, underline the name.

Jargon   It is tempting to use a pseudo-technical vocabulary to make things sound more important. But it usually has the effect of making the writer look immature. There is no need to talk about an 'interface' when one means a 'border' or 'frontier', and a word like 'exponential' can usually be replaced with a simple word like 'fast'.

Kind of, sort of   While we may speak of 'those kind of trees', technically we should write 'this kind of trees' or 'these kinds of trees'. 'This kind of trees' sounds wrong because of the mismatch between the singular 'this' and the plural noun 'trees'. It seems better to find a way round this and write 'trees of this kind'. Exactly the same point holds good for 'sort of'.

Lords, Ladies and Gentlemen   It is important to address someone in the correct manner. At university, for example, most of the lecturers are either Professor or Doctor. If a university lecturer, a Dr Watson, for example, receives a letter from a student that begins 'Dear Mrs Watson', she isn't going to be offended because you have failed to address her in the correct manner. But she is going to assume that you are a bit dim, in that you have so signally failed to grasp a basic convention of writing. You just cannot afford to make this kind of careless mistake: write, read what you have written, think and check, and alter if necessary.

Mumbai   This in a way is exactly the same point as the one we have just made. The Indian city that used to be called Bombay is now called Mumbai. In a similar way, the city that people in the West used to call Peking is now called Beijing. There are good reasons for these changes; the old names smacked of colonialism, of Europeans imposing an identity on the rest of the world. When you are writing you should be aware of matters like this. Stop, think and check. You might say, 'it doesn't matter if I call it Bombay'. Our response is that continuing to refer to Mumbai as Bombay is racist and offensive. It is, in a variety of ways, a lazy, thoughtless mistake that betrays a lack of intelligence.

Neither   'Neither' refers to two people or two things, but, like 'either', it should be followed by the singular verb form: 'neither of them is here'. And just as we pair 'either' with 'or' ('either you are coming or you are not'), so we pair 'neither' with 'nor': 'neither a girl nor a boy was to be seen'.

Oxymoron   Some grammatical terms, such as 'gerund', are frightening, but there are other words that we use in relation to words that describe some of the more amusing and entertaining aspects of language. One of the best is 'oxymoron'. This is when two words with apparently opposite meanings are combined, such as 'awfully good' and 'terribly nice'. Occasionally you might hear a football commentator refer to a 'fair foul', or someone say that X is 'blooming well dead'. The DJ 'Fatboy Slim' obviously knows about oxymorons as well as music. Writers are particularly fond of oxymorons: Shakespeare, in *Romeo and Juliet*, writes of a 'loving hate', Milton of a 'darkness visible', while Tennyson, in *Lancelot and Elaine*, writes how 'faith unfaithful kept him falsely true'.

Pronunciation   The English language was invented to make fools of most of us by not always spelling words as they sound. We often speak of the 'prisner' instead of the 'prisoner'; we know about the 'pharaohs' but they sound like the 'fairose'; and we send MPs to 'parlament' but spell it 'parliament'. The list of such things is long enough to catch most people eventually, but you need to be alert to such dangers, especially in situations such as lectures where the temptation is to assume new words are spelt the way they sound.

Quotation marks   If you use quotation marks in an essay, stick either to single or double throughout, except where you have a quotation within a quotation. Let's say you are citing a critic writing about *Hamlet* and decide to use the following quotation: 'Hamlet's soliloquy "To be or not to be" is at once the centre of the play and also a commentary on its theme of noble murder.' Here the double quotation marks are used within the single ones being used for the essay as a whole. If you opt for double quotations as your default style, then you use single quotation marks inside the double ones.

Reference works   There are, quite literally, thousands of books about language and all its many aspects. We have already mentioned some of the works most often cited, including David Crystal's *Cambridge Encyclopedia of the English Language* (Cambridge: Cambridge University Press, 1987) and H. W. Fowler's *Modern English Usage* (1926), now available as *The New Fowler's Modern English Usage* (Oxford: Clarendon Press, 1996). Excellent in every way is R. L. Trask's *The Penguin Guide to Punctuation* (London: Penguin, 1997), while Loreto Todd's *Cassell's Guide to Punctuation* (London: Cassell, 1995) offers much useful advice and information. *The Economist Style Guide* (London: Profile, 1986) is similarly informative. Other resources include Melvyn Bragg's *The Adventure of English: The Biography of a Language* (London: Hodder & Stoughton, 2003), which was also a television series in 2003.

Spelling   George Bernard Shaw pointed out that the word 'fish' could be spelt 'ghoti': the 'gh' as in 'rough'; the 'o' as in 'women'; and the 'ti' of 'nation'. There are tricks that can help sort out how words are spelt. One is to sound words out carefully, emphasising each syllable or sound element: say 'Feb/ru/ary', not '*Febuary'; 'gov/ern/ment', not '*govenment'. But, ultimately, there is no way of avoiding the effort involved in getting to grips with the oddities of English spelling.

Typos   These are the little mistakes we all make when typing. Use the Spellcheck to check what you have written. But you also need to print out and then proof-read and correct what you have written. It is almost impossible to concentrate on a computer screen in the kind of way that you will have to do when checking what you have written. At university, remember that the difference between an unchecked and unrevised essay and a polished, fully checked essay might be the difference between an Upper Second and a First Class degree.

Unnecessary words   'Cutbacks' means 'cuts'. 'Large-scale' means 'big'. 'Weather conditions' means 'weather'. It's quite informative, in fact, to listen to a weather forecast on television to see how many extra words are used to pad things out and to add fake weightiness to the forecast. 'There will be rain in the evening part of the day' means 'There will be rain in the evening'. 'Temperature values of around ten degrees', means 'Temperatures around ten degrees'. Look at the opening of the last essay you wrote. How many words can you cut without doing any damage – and probably managing to improve things?

Verbosity and verbiage   Using ten words where one will do. Don't do it. Say more by saying less.

Which and that   This is something that drives people mad when they check what they have written on Microsoft Word. If you have written 'which' it often asks you if you mean 'that', and when you change it to 'that', it asks you if you mean 'which'. Generally speaking, use 'that' in a defining clause: 'The car that I used to own'. Use 'which' in a descriptive clause, and then put that bit of the sentence between commas: 'My car, which has served me reliably for years, has finally conked out.'

Xerox   There are lots of brand names that have been absorbed into general usage. We use a capital letter when we talk about the product – e.g. the Xerox machine – but we use lower case when we use the verb, talking about the activity they perform. For example, 'I'll xerox that document, and then I'll do the hoovering.'

Yolk and yoke Homophones are words that sound alike but mean different things: 'sort' and 'sought'; taut' and 'taught'; 'towed' and 'toed'; 'there and their'. This last is an old favourite for confusion. A remedy is to remember that 'there' is the opposite of 'here'. Other pairs, however, have to be learnt: the principal of your college may be a person of principles, but make sure you don't make him/her faint by fighting a duel – or should that be 'feint' and 'dual'? And whatever you do, don't confuse 'it's' and 'its'. Yolk is what you get in an egg, whereas yoke is used on oxen.

Zeitgeist *Zeitgeist* means 'spirit of the times'. When a foreign word is used in an English sentence it is italicised, or if you are using a word-processor you might choose to underline the foreign word rather than put it in italics. When a foreign word or phrase has become so much a part of English that we barely notice it as having its origins elsewhere, we use ordinary roman, as in 'status quo'.

▶ 99 Don't be afraid to break the rules

The best writers nearly always break the rules in one way or another. The strict rules include such things as not starting a sentence with 'And' or 'But' as these are conjunctions and should be used to join sentences or units together. But there is no real harm in occasionally starting a sentence this way. Similarly, fragments. These are sentences without verbs, but where the sense is clear and where extra words would simply add weight but little substance. For example, the two-word sentence we have just used is a fragment: 'Similarly, fragments.' This could be changed into a full sentence – 'The same holds good for fragments' – and many would insist on this, but you will come across examples of fragments, even in the most correct of books, when the writer has judged that this will add something to the texture of the writing. Of course, if you break the rules without knowing it you are likely to run into trouble, but the more you learn about language, the more you will come to realise how flexible it is and how it can be made to serve different purposes. Some rules are too basic to be broken, but it is possible to write sentences in all kinds of different ways in order to stress different meanings.

One old-fashioned rule that nearly everybody breaks is that of not ending sentences with a preposition: 'She carried on with her sport of rock-climbing which she had been warned against.' But often you can recast sentences so as to avoid any ungainliness or ambiguity when prepositions are placed next to one another: 'Rock concerts in New York are a wholly different matter from in Basingstoke' reads more easily as 'Rock concerts in New York are a wholly different matter from those staged in Basingstoke'. As with all such points, the test is whether your meaning is clear and whether you are in control of your writing and its effect on your readers.

▶ 100 But even if you get it all wrong, you can still become president of the United States

We end with some famous 'Bushisms', proof that even the most powerful man in the world can be defeated by syntax and vocabulary. Or perhaps they are evidence that even language cannot fight back against those who make it more confusing than it is:

> I think there is a Trojan horse lurking in the weeds trying to pull a fast one on the American people.

> They misunderestimated me.

> Families is where our nation finds hope, where wings take dream.

> I know it is hard for you to put food on your family.

> You teach a child to read, and he or her will be able to pass a literacy test.

If you can see that there is something just a little bit wrong in each of these sentences, you have an ear for correct usage; you might also realise that altering just a word or two would transform each faulty sentence into a polished, even inspiring, political soundbite. The chances are that, in just about every sentence you write, changing a word or two, or tinkering with punctuation, could achieve a similar transformation. It is a case of appreciating the difference between thinking out loud, and the tiny degree of extra care required in writing.

Glossary

The list that follows covers the basic terms used in this book together with a number of other terms that you may come across. The main parts of speech are nouns, verbs, pronouns, adverbs, adjectives, conjunctions, prepositions, interjections and articles. Modern grammarians, however, prefer to talk about word classes or groups rather than parts of speech; in addition, they tend to describe grammar as a system of language rather than invoking the traditional idea of a set of rules.

Abstract noun   A noun that names an idea or state or quality that does not have a physical (concrete) existence: *love*, *worry*, *generosity*. Abstract nouns also describe actions: *singing*, *thinking*, *walking*.

Active voice (active verb)   A transitive verb is one that takes an object. The verb can be put either in the active voice – 'The fire *destroyed* the house' – or in the passive voice: 'The house *was destroyed* by fire.'

Adjective   An adjective is a describing word; it usually modifies (that is, affects the meaning of) a noun: *green* trees, *yellow* bananas.

Adverb   An adverb qualifies a verb (run *quickly*), or an adjective (*extremely* hot) or an adverb (*very* quickly), or a sentence.

Agreement   In grammar words have to agree or show concord. The commonest agreement is between subject and verb: *I run*, but *she runs*. The subject and verb agree here because they use the same person and number. **I are* is wrong because 'are' is a plural verb and therefore agrees with 'we' or 'you' or 'they' but not 'I'.

Article   There are just two articles – the definite article (the word *the*), and the indefinite article (the word *a* or *an*). Modern grammarians call these 'determiners', along with words such as *all, both, this, few, little*.

Auxiliary verb   Sometimes called 'helping verbs'. The primary ones are the verbs *be, have* and *do*. They are used in combination with main verbs to form various tenses: *I have eaten.*

A second group of auxiliaries are called **modal auxiliaries**: *can, could, may, might, must, ought to, shall, should, will, would,*

Clause   A clause is a group of words that has a subject and a finite verb. There are two basic types: main clauses and subordinate clauses. There are also non-finite clauses: 'She loved *to sing songs.'*

Collective noun   A noun that names a group or a collection of things or people: *team, herd, family, army, audience.*

Complement   A word or phrase used to complete a sentence: 'She is *a nice person.'* 'They are *really good friends.'*

Concrete noun   A noun that names something that is tangible or real: *tree, woman, car, house.*

Conjunction   A word that serves to link other words or parts of a clause or sentences together. There are two main types: co-ordinating conjunctions and subordinating conjunctions.

Contraction   This refers to the shortening of a word, usually by omitting a vowel, or by combining some elements: *can't* for 'cannot'; *I'm* for 'I am'.

Co-ordinating conjunction   A word that joins two clauses together: *and, but, or, for, yet, nor, so.* These are the only words that can join main clauses (sentences) together.

Definite article   The only definite article is the word *the.*

Demonstrative pronouns   The demonstrative pronouns are *this, that, these,* and *those.*

Ellipses   Three dots used to indicate the omission of a word or words from a quotation: 'Shall I compare thee to a . . . day?' There is no need to use ellipses at the start and end of a quotation.

Figurative language   Language that is not literally true. Figurative language uses figures of speech such as metaphor and simile: 'She shattered all my dreams'; 'My dreams were shattered like a window.'

Finite verb   All sentences must contain a finite verb. To be finite a verb must agree with (or match) its subject 'He walks oddly.' The verb is called 'finite' because it is limited: it agrees in number and person with its subject.

Finite verbs can be in the present (*walks*) or past (*walked*) or future tense. The future tense is formed by using the modal verbs *will* or *shall* ('I will ring you'), or the verb 'go' plus the 'to' or infinitive form of the verb: 'I am going to ring you.'

Gerund   This is the *ing* form of verbs – e.g. 'walking', 'singing'. When it is used as a noun it is called a 'gerund' or 'verbal noun': '*Walking* is good for you.' 'I like *dancing.*'

Indefinite article   The indefinite articles are *a* and *an*. The word 'article' simply means 'the name for'.

Indefinite pronouns   These are words like *somebody*, *no one*, *something*, *all*, *most*, *several* – that is, words used where there is no definite reference to a particular person or quantity.

Independent clause   The same as a main clause. 'Independent' refers to the fact that the clause can stand on its own as a sentence.

Indirect speech   What someone says is direct speech: *He said, 'Don't shout.'* When it is reported it becomes indirect speech: *He told me not to shout.*

Infinitive verb form   This is the 'to' form of verbs: *to think*. It remains unchanged or uninflected.

Inflection   Many words change in order to indicate different tenses or numbers. For example, the past tense of the verb *see* is *saw*; the plural of *girl* is *girls*. English is not, however, a heavily inflected language, unlike French or German. For example, in English the future tense (*I will love you*) is created by combining the verb *love* with the auxiliary verb *will*. In other languages the verb 'love' is inflected, with different endings added to it.

Interjection   An exclamation – usually a word or a short phrase: *Cool! Ouch! Goodness me!*

Interrogative pronouns   These are used to ask a question. They are: *which*, *who*, *whom*, *whose*.

Intransitive verb   A verb that does not have an object: *Jane laughed loudly. The boys ran quickly.* Some verbs are always intransitive: *arrive*, *come*, *digress*, *creep*, *ache*. Many verbs can be used either transitively or intransitively.

Irregular verbs   Verbs that do not form their past tense in the usual way by adding *ed*. For example, the past tense of 'take' is 'took', while the past participle is 'taken'. The most important irregular verb is the verb to 'be', with its present tense of 'I am', past tense of 'I was' and past participle of 'been'.

Main clause   The same as an independent clause. A main clause is a clause that has a subject and a finite verb and can stand on its own as a sentence. Two or more main clauses can be joined together using a co-ordinating conjunction to form a compound sentence.

Mood   Verbs can be in one of three moods: indicative, imperative and subjunctive. The indicative is the commonest and describes verbs making a statement: *She went home. The house was empty.* The imperative mood is used for making commands: *Go home!* The subjunctive mood is used to express uncertainty or wishes or doubt: *If he were guilty, he would be in jail.*

   Sentences, however, can be in one of four moods: the declarative, which is the same as the indicative; the imperative, the subjunctive, and, additionally, the interrogative, used for asking questions: *Do you believe in ghosts?*

Non-finite verb   The four non-finite forms of a verb are the base form (*run*), the 'to' or infinitive form (*to run*), the present participle (*running*), and the past participle (*ran*). Non-finite means the verb does not change its form.

Noun   A noun is the name of a thing or a person. There are four basic types: common or concrete nouns (*book, star, dog*), abstract nouns naming something that cannot be seen (*anger, loyalty, health*), collective nouns referring to groups (*family, flock*), and proper nouns or proper names – the names given to a person or place (*John, Jane, Europe*), or days of the week and months of the year.

Number   The technical term for whether something is singular or plural.

Object   The object in a sentence is the person or thing affected by the verb: *The boy hit the ball. The lorry destroyed the house.* Both 'the ball' and 'the house' are direct objects. A sentence must have a subject and a finite verb, but it does not have to have an object: *She sings excellently.* Here, 'excellently' is a complement, not an object.

   As well as direct objects (DO), there are also indirect objects (IO): *She gave him* [IO] *the ball* [DO]. The indirect object is usually the person receiving the object.

Paragraph   This is not strictly a grammatical term. It means a group of sentences on the same topic, set out in a group on the page. The first line of a new paragraph, apart from the first paragraph of an essay, is usually indented.

Passive voice (passive verb) A passive verb is where something is done to the subject of the sentence: 'The car *was driven* by the woman.' The key to the passive is the use of a form of the verb *to be* (here, 'was') and the past participle of another verb (here, 'driven').

Past participle The past participle of most verbs is the *ed* form: *walked, talked*. Irregular verbs such as 'do' and 'go', however, do not add *ed* in this way but change to '*done*', '*gone*'.

Person In looking at verbs and personal pronouns a distinction is made between the first person ('I'), the second person ('you'/'thou') and the third person ('he', 'she', 'it'). These are the singular forms. The plural forms are 'we', 'you' and 'they'. The second person plural is the same as the second person singular – 'you'.

Personal pronouns These take the place of nouns. They can be the subject or object of a sentence. In the sentence 'I want a job', the personal pronoun 'I' is the subject; in the sentence 'She told me', the pronoun 'me' is the object. More technically, the personal pronoun 'I' is in what is called the 'subjective case', while 'me' is the 'objective case' of the first person singular.

	Singular	*Plural*
First person	I/me	we/us
Second person	you/you thou/thee	you/you
Third person	he/him she/her it/it	they/them they/them they/them

Phrase A group of words without a verb.

Possessive pronouns These are used to show ownership or possession or who something belongs to. They are:

	Singular	*Plural*
First person	mine	ours
Second person	yours thine	yours
Third person	his hers its	theirs theirs theirs

Some grammars also include here 'my', 'your', 'thy', 'his', 'her', 'our', and 'their'. More traditional grammars call these possessive adjectives, while recent grammars classify them as possessive determiners.

Predicate   A sentence has two main parts: the subject and the predicate. The predicate is everything apart from the subject.

Prefix   An addition to the front of a word that changes its meaning: for example, 'appear' becomes '*dis*appear' or '*re*appear'.

Preposition   Usually a short word such as *to* or *at* that serves to relate two words. Prepositions are usually placed before nouns.

Present participle   The present participle of a verb is the *ing* form: *reading*, *writing*.

Pronoun   A pronoun is, generally, a word that replaces or stands for a noun. There are six basic types of pronoun: demonstrative, indefinite, interrogative, personal, possessive and relative. Pronouns thus constitute a significant number of small groups.

Proper noun   A proper noun (sometimes called a 'proper name') is a noun that is the name of a person, place or thing: *London*, *Jane*, *Cardiff University*, the *British Library*. Proper nouns always have a capital letter.

Punctuation marks   The various marks used to divide up writing into sentences or clauses and to indicate meaning.

Reflexive pronouns   These are the words that refer back to the subject of a clause. They are:

	Singular	*Plural*
First person	myself	ourselves
Second person	{ yourself thyself	yourself
Third person	himself herself itself	themselves themselves themselves

Relative pronouns   These are the words *who*, *whom*, *whose*, *which* and *that*. These words, apart from 'that', also function as interrogative pronouns.

Sentences   All sentences, to be sentences, must have a subject and a finite verb. There are three main types of sentence: simple, compound and complex. A simple sentence consists of a single grammatical subject and a single finite verb. In other words it consists of one main clause. A compound sentence consists of two or more main clauses joined together. A complex sentence consists of one or more main clauses and one or more subordinate clauses.

Standard English   The type of (educated) English found in grammar books and which serves as the norm for spoken and written English.

Subject   A sentence can be divided into two parts – the subject and the predicate. The grammatical subject is the noun or pronoun or noun phrase that governs or determines the main verb. ('Subject' here does not mean 'theme' or 'topic'.)

Subordinate clause   A group of words containing a verb but not able to stand on its own as a sentence. It is subordinate because it depends on the main clause to make sense.

Subordinating conjunction   This introduces a subordinate clause and includes words like *that, which, because, since, although, after* and *unless*.

Suffix   An addition at the end of a word that changes its meaning: for example, 'hope' becomes 'hopeful' or 'hopeless'.

Syntax   The arrangement of words to form sentences – more simply, the structure of sentences.

Tenses   The basic tenses are past, present and future. These are shown by the verbs in sentences: 'I *walked*', 'she *walks*', 'he *will walk*'. There are, however, other tenses:

- Present perfect: 'she *has gone* away'

- Past perfect: 'he *had gone* back'

- Future perfect: 'we *will have* finished'

- Present progressive (the verb 'to be' plus the present participle): 'I *am running*'

- Past progressive: 'he *was walking*'

- Future progressive: 'I *will be leaving*'

- Present perfect progressive: 'I *have been waiting*'

- Past perfect progressive: 'I *had been waiting*'

Topic sentence   This is the main (often the first) sentence of a paragraph. It sets up the subject of the paragraph.

Transitive verb   Many verbs can be either transitive or intransitive. A transitive verb is one that takes an object: *The ball hit him.*

Verb   A verb is a doing word – it describes an action. Verbs have a number of forms: the base form (*walk*), the infinitive form (*to walk*), the present participle (*walking*) and the past participle (*walked*).

Full Contents Guide

3   Writing Correct and Convincing Sentences

**4   Punctuating a Sentence: Commas, Colons and
     Semicolons**

5   Avoidable Errors

Index